Three Plays *by*
Padraic Colum

Three Plays by

Padraic Colum

An Chomhairle Ealaíon Series of Irish Authors
Number Three

Three Plays
by
Padraic Colum

1963
ALLEN FIGGIS
Dublin

V138326

For permission to publish or reproduce the plays in this collection,
acknowledgement is made to the owner of copyright therein,
Padraic Colum.

Application for the right of performing
these plays or reading them in public should be made to :

The Authors Guild of Ireland, Ltd.,
1, Clare Street, Dublin 2.

Made and printed in the Republic of Ireland by

BROWNE & NOLAN LTD., DUBLIN

PREFACE

These three plays were written between my twenty-first and twenty-eighth birthdays. But looking at this statement I have to say that it is not altogether factual: a play written at the early date, " Broken Soil," became one of the plays in this collection " The Fiddler's House," both this and " Thomas Muskerry " were revised to some extent after their first production. " The Land " remains as it was first produced.

And now I find that to be informative about these plays —and a Preface should be informative—I have to write a little history. The theatre they were written for had its rise in a nationalist movement. There were the clubs, Cuman na nGaedheal with its feminine counterpart, Inginidh na hEireann (Daughters of Ireland). These undertook to produce plays that would forward the cause of " Irish Ireland," and because there were associated with them rather obliquely two men who were really of the theatre, Willie Fay and Frank Fay, these, or rather one club, Inginidh formed the rudiments of an Irish theatre.

Influencing this formation was a movement that had run its course. This was the Irish Literary Theatre in which W. B. Yeats, George Moore and Edward Martyn were standard-bearers. Their aim was to produce in Dublin, at a sort of annual festival, plays of literary distinction written by Irish authors; but as Dublin had no available actors or directors at the time, these plays had to be directed and acted by personnel from the London theatres. After the third annual production the Irish Literary Theatre came to an end. It left a certain excitement and a certain ambition in its wake: moreover, its last production included a short play in Irish acted by a Gaelic League group. More important than the players was the director: he was Willie

1

Fay. Then, with his brother Frank, an elocution instructor —a remarkable elocution instructor, I should say—he became a helper in the Clubs' dramatics.

The "Daughters of Ireland" had taken to public representations. These were very ingenuous *tableaux vivants*. And what were *tableaux vivants*, our cinema-goers may well enquire. They were statuesque groups introduced by some familiar piece of music, and holding their pose for some minutes—an elementary show in which costume, music and striking appearance were ingredients. These easily staged *tableaux* the "Daughters of Ireland" used to advance the "Irish Ireland" idea. Moore's melodies were ideal material. Someone at a piano played, let us say, "Avenging and Bright fell the Swift Sword of Erin," and thereupon a scanty but appreciative audience beheld a *tableau* in which one could distinguish a maidenly Deirdre, a gallant Naisi, a threatening King Conor. Or it might be "The Harp that once through Tara's Halls," and the audience saw a colourful company being enlivened by a harper. Under such auspices my intermittent dramatic career began. I was in an audience that witnessed "Silent, O Moyle, be the Roar of thy Waters." I felt there should be words to give life to the pathos of children transformed by an enchantress step-mother; my mind was already on plays. I began a one act play in verse, "The Children of Lir" and sent it to the secretary of Inginidh, Maire Quinn. Invited to their ambitious production of Alice Milligan's "Flight of Red Hugh" I was introduced to the Director and principal players, Willie and Frank Fay.

With this production the acting members of "The Daughters of Ireland" graduated from the *tableaux* stage. They now became attached to the Fays' company of amateur players and continued to receive instruction from the brothers, the more extraordinary parts being given by

2

that enthusiast for speech, Frank Fay. I was allowed the privilege of attending rehearsals and found myself with the Fay veterans, young actors, notably Dudley Digges, the yet untried actresses, Máire Nic Shiubhlaigh (Maire Walker) and Maire Quinn. The ghost of the Irish Literary Theatre was still around. Its last production, " Diarmuid and Grania " had been attended by Standish O'Grady and A.E. Both, but for different reasons, were outraged by what they saw—the degradation of the Irish heroic image. A.E.'s recoil was productive: he started to write a play in which the heroic image would not be defaced; it was the first of our three " Deirdres." Frank Fay discovered it in Standish O'Grady's "All Ireland Review "—two acts of it, for the third was still to be written. The elocutionist was fascinated by the unusual dramatic speech; he got permission to put in rehearsal the two acts which had appeared. Fay's company was working at an English farce, " His Last Legs." That disposed of, an enthusiastic company took on " Deirdre." A.E. gave them the last act and brought his prophetic presence to rehearsals. Then Maud Gonne brought W. B. Yeats. The dramatist of " The Countess Cathleen " and the part dramatist of " Diarmuid and Grania " was seeking re-entrance to the theatre. He approved of " Deirdre " as seen and heard in rehearsal and gave Fay the play he had just finished, " Cathleen ni Houlihan." With these two plays the company felt equipped to go before an audience that had welcomed Douglas Hyde's play after the performance of " Diarmuid and Grania." Their production in the Carmelite Hall in 1902 launched the Irish Theatre.

New forces were felt, new plays were offered to what had become the National Theatre Society. A hall for rehearsals and productions was found in Camden Street next a grocery shop. In the Camden Street hall the National Theatre Society became coherent and purposeful.

3

"The King's Threshold" was rehearsed here: under Frank Fay's tutoring, the cast which included practically all the members became famed speakers of verse. New members came in from Inginidh, foremost among them Sara Allgood. Then Maire Garvey. Honor Lavelle who had come in with the "Deirdre" rehearsals showed style in the first parts she was given. Yeats put before the Society two short plays by an unheard of writer, John M. Synge—unexpected kind of plays. Performances were given, but the location, unattractiveness and discomfort of the hall kept the occasional audience sparse. There were discussions led by Yeats and the Fays. There was training through rehearsals. As for myself, I learnt how to bring characters on and get them off the stage, how to write a speech that would mean something to an audience.

The composition of the vital group that gathered in the Camden Street hall has to be considered. In some the "Irish Ireland" ideology was dominant, in others not so dominant. The production of "In the Shadow of the Glen" was decided on and this decision brought about the loss of two important members of the Society, Dudley Digges and the actress who had the lead in "Deirdre," Maire Quinn (they became Mr. and Mrs. Dudley Digges). Why? They felt the play let the Irish country people down. In those days it was an article of faith that the country people were the heart, soul and voice of Ireland. And there was another crisis. Cuman na nGaedheal offered a prize for a one act play that would be propaganda against enlistment in the British Army. I won the prize, and "The Saxon Shillin'" was offered to the National Theatre Society for production. Fay declined to put it on. There were whispers of Castle influence. Maud Gonne and Arthur Griffith who were members of the Society took their leave with denunciation of myself for submitting to the higher-ups. These happenings show the

4

strains that were in the Society: there was a political group and a group that was not so political. After this I wrote a play that was acceptable to the whole Society, " Broken Soil " (" The Fiddler's House ").

It was put on after the first production of Synge's " In the Shadow of the Glen ". Both were given in a bleak hall in Molesworth Street and to a sparse audience. " In the Shadow of the Glen " got the tribute of a hiss. " Broken Soil " was made endearing to some of the audience by the playing of Frank Fay as Conn Hourican and Máire Nic Shiubhlaigh as Maire Hourican.

By this time the National Theatre Society had something of a repertoire and it was decided to accept an invitation from the Irish Literary Society to produce their plays in London. Yeats and Lady Gregory tacitly disapproved of having " Broken Soil " among the plays offered: it was immature, they said, and they were right in saying it. The company insisted on putting it on; it had come out of their own endeavours they declared. In London (1904) the productions got glowing notices from the foremost critics. The quietude of the players, the freshness of their idiom, the beauty of their speech made a real impression. " Broken Soil " had a share in these acclamations.

The strains in the Society developed. It was a co-operative society with everyone in the original group having a say as to the plays to be produced and the policy to be followed. Newcomers to our stage hadn't any influence. And now a theatre, actual premises, were offered to the Society by an English devotee of the theatre, Miss Horniman. But a tune was being called. The original Society was to be dissolved and a directorate consisting of W. B. Yeats, Willie Fay, Lady Gregory and J. M. Synge put in charge. This meant the deposition of the political-minded members and of a very sincere element who wanted a really democratic organization. Yeats and

Willie Fay were for a theatre directed from the top. After a show-down in which they were out-voted, members who wanted nationalism in the theatre and those who favoured democratic control left the organization. I went with them. In parenthesis I should observe that newcomers, fine actors though they were, had no franchise in the Society.

Before our departure the premises, the Abbey Theatre, had been gained. My mature play, "The Land" was produced there. The last that the united Society did. It pleased an audience who wanted a theatre that would have political orientation; as the people who fought the Land War were shown as coming into their own, this was felt as a chapter in the re-conquest, and it had the approval of the hundred per cent nationalists. It was accepted, too, by the literary coteries. Indeed "The Land" was the first popular success the Irish Theatre had. There was another visit to London with a success equal to the first. The split and the directorate ensued. Only a few of the originating group were left to carry on in the Abbey Theatre, but they included Willie Fay, Frank Fay, and Sara Allgood as well as new members who had been trained in the united Society.

"The Fiddler's House" was produced by the group which had left the Abbey Theatre and named themselves "The Theatre of Ireland." Later the third play in this collection, "Thomas Muskerry" was given production in the Abbey, but this did not involve my return to the theatre.

And now for some discussion—no, for some reflection on the three plays which the Arts Council has done me the honour to publish after so many changes in the social history that they came out of.

The passion for the land that motivates the first play is not likely to be responded to in days when farms are being abandoned and when the men who knew the oppression of landlordism as Murtagh Cosgar and Martin Douras did are not to be met with in the flesh. If staged these days " The Land " would have to be played as an historical piece and for character parts. However, another issue could give relevancy—the revolt of the young against parental possessiveness. In the first production (1905), " The Land " had Willie Fay and Frank Fay as Murtagh Cosgar and Martin Douras, Arthur Sinclair as Cornelius Douras, Sara Allgood as Sally, Frank Walker as Matt Cosgar, Maire Garvey as Ellen Douras—a memorable cast indeed.

" The Fiddler's House " was produced in a hall in the Rotunda in 1907. The motive in its early version, "Broken Soil " was simply ' the call of the road.' It became " The Fiddler's House " when a real conflict was seen as developing in it, the conflict between father and daughter in which reconciliation came when Maire Hourican becomes aware that she, too, has the vagrant in her. Later, when produced in New York by Augustin Duncan, something else in her character was made explicit. Her recoil from her lover is due to her fear of masculine possessiveness—a recoil not extraordinary in a girl brought up in the Irish countryside. The cast in this production included Máire Nic Shiubhlaigh who had given our theatricalism radiance from the time of the *tableaux vivants,* Conn Hourican was played by a sensitive actor who was seldom seen on the Dublin stage, Joseph Goggin. He had another part outside the theatre that fixes him in our minds: his was the model for the poet's features in the Mangan memorial in St. Stephen's Green.

Since the first production of " Thomas Muskerry " (1910) changes have been made in it. As it exists in the present text two scenes have been added; they are in the interest of pausing, and timing. The Master of Garrisowen Workhouse in the original was given too swift a descent

7

from the Master's office to the pauper's bed. It was given a very affecting production. Arthur Sinclair whom I regard as one of the great actors of our time had the lead, and there were Sara Allgood, Maire O'Neill and J. M. Kerrigan (who doubled, giving sharp delineation to both parts). Kerrigan was—and I hope that in distant Hollywood he still is—an actor whose improvised lines improve a text. The performances of "Thomas Muskerry" were well attended by the intellectuals of Dublin Castle. I remember J. M. Kerrigan as the nameless pauper with the sweeping brush coming up to the footlights and muttering, "And who do we have before us now? No one but Castle hacks."

After "Thomas Muskerry" I wrote no more for the Irish stage. (A one-act melodrama, "The Betrayal" is marginal). Perhaps this was because the attraction had dimmed. Or perhaps it was because that after the man of the land, the artist, the official, there were no other types in the countryside I knew that I wanted to make articulate.

Padraic Colum

Dublin, 1963.

The Land

A play in three acts

Characters

MURTAGH COSGAR, *a farmer.*
MATT, *his son.*
SALLY, *his daughter.*
MARTIN DOURAS, *a farmer.*
CORNELIUS, *his son.*
ELLEN, *his daughter.*
A group of men.
A group of boys and girls.

The scene is laid in the Irish Midlands. The action is contemporary with the stage-presentation.

10

ACT ONE

The interior of Murtagh Cosgar's. It is a large flagged kitchen. The entrance is at back right. The half-door is closed. There is a room-door a pace below the entrance, and below that a harness-rack. The fire-place occupies nearly the whole of the left. Another room-door above it. The dresser is at back, and a little window to the left of it. There is a bench outside, and a corner of it can be seen when the half-door is open.

It is the afternoon of a May day. SALLY COSGAR is kneeling near the entrance chopping up cabbage-leaves with a kitchen knife. She is a girl of twenty-five, dark, heavily-built, with the expression of a half-awakened creature. She is coarsely dressed, and has a sacking apron. She is quick at work, and rapid and impetuous in speech. She is talking to herself.

cf. Pegeen. Different dimension.

SALLY : Oh, you may go on grunting, yourself and your litter, it won't put me a bit past my own time. You oul' black baste of a sow, sure I'm slaving to you all the spring. We'll be getting rid of yourself and your litter soon enough, and may the devil get you when we lose you.

> (CORNELIUS *comes to the door. He is a tall young man with a slight stoop. His manners are solemn, and his expression somewhat vacant.*)

CORNELIUS : Good morrow, Sally. May you have the good of the day. (*He comes in.*)

SALLY (*impetuously*) : Ah, God reward you, Cornelius Douras, for coming in. I'm that busy keeping food to a sow and a litter of pigs that I couldn't get beyond the gate to see anyone.

11

CORNELIUS (*solemnly*) : You're a good girl, Sally. You're not like some I know. There are girls in this parish who never put hands to a thing till evening, when the boys do be coming in. Then they begin to stir themselves the way they'll be thought busy and good about the house.

SALLY (*pleased, and beginning to chop again with renewed energy*) : Oh, it's true indeed for you, Cornelius. There are girls that be decking themselves, and sporting themselves, all day.

CORNELIUS : I may say that I come over to your father's, Murtagh Cosgar's house, this morning, thinking to meet the men.

SALLY : What men, Cornelius Douras?

CORNELIUS : Them that are going to meet the landlord's people with an offer for the land. We're not buying ourselves, unfortunately, but this is a great day— the day of the redemption, my father calls it—and I'd like to have some hand in the work if it was only to say a few words to the men.

SALLY : It's a wonder, Martin, your father isn't on the one errand with you.

CORNELIUS : We came out together, but the priest stopped father and we on the road. Father Bartley wanted his advice, I suppose. Ah, it's a pity the men won't have someone like my father with them! He was in gaol for the cause. Besides, he's a well-discoursed man, and a reading man, and, moreover, a man with a classical knowledge of English, Latin, and the Hibernian vernacular.

(MARTIN DOURAS *comes in. He is a man of about sixty, with a refined, scholarly look. His manner is subdued and nervous. He has a stoop, and is clean-shaven.*)

12

CORNELIUS : I was just telling Sally here what a great day it is, Father.

MARTIN DOURAS : Ay, it's a great day, no matter what our own troubles may be. I should be going home again. (*He takes a newspaper out of his pocket, and leaves it on the table.*)

CORNELIUS : Wait for the men, Father.

MARTIN DOURAS : Maybe they'll be here soon. Is Murtagh in, Sally? (CORNELIUS *takes the paper up, and begins to read it.*)

SALLY : He's down at the bottoms, Martin.

MARTIN DOURAS : He's going to Arvach Fair, maybe.

SALLY : He is in troth.

MARTIN DOURAS : I'll be asking him for a lift. He'll be going to the fair when he comes back from the lawyer's, I suppose?

SALLY : Ay, he'll be going to-night. (*She gathers the chopped cabbage into her apron, and goes to the door.*)

SALLY (*at the door*) : Cornelius!
          (CORNELIUS *puts down the paper, and goes to the door.* SALLY *goes out.*)

MARTIN DOURAS : Cornelius! (CORNELIUS *goes to* MARTIN.)

SALLY (*Outside*) : Cornelius, give me a hand with this. (CORNELIUS *turns again.*)

MARTIN DOURAS : Cornelius, I want to speak to you. (CORNELIUS *goes to him.*)

MARTIN DOURAS : There is something on my mind, Cornelius.

CORNELIUS : What is it, Father?

MARTIN DOURAS : It's about our Ellen. Father Bartley gave me news for her. "I've heard of a school that'll suit Ellen," says he. "It's in the County Leitrim."

CORNELIUS : If it was in Dublin itself, Ellen is qualified to take it on. And won't it be grand to have one of our family teaching in a school?

13

MARTIN DOURAS (*with a sigh*) : I wouldn't stand in her
way, Cornelius; I wouldn't stand in her way. But
won't it be a poor thing for an old man like me to
have no one to discourse with in the long evenings?
For when I'm talking with you, Cornelius, I feel like
a boy who lends back all the marbles he's won, and
plays again, just for the sake of the game.

CORNELIUS : We were in dread of Ellen going to America
at one time, and then she went in for the school. Now
Matt Cosgar may keep her from the school. Maybe
we won't have to go further than this house to see
Ellen.

MARTIN DOURAS : I'm hoping it'll be like that; but I'm in
dread that Murtagh Cosgar will never agree to it.
He's a hard man to deal with. Still Murtagh and
myself will be on the long road to-night, and we
might talk of it. I'm afeard of Ellen going.

CORNELIUS (*at the door*) : It's herself that's coming here,
Father.

MARTIN DOURAS : Maybe she has heard the news and is
coming to tell us.

(ELLEN *comes in. She has a shawl over her head
which she lays aside. She is about twenty-five,
slightly built, nervous, emotional.*)

ELLEN : Is it only ourselves that's here?

MARTIN DOURAS : Only ourselves. Did you get any news
to bring you over, Ellen?

ELLEN : No news. It was the shine of the day that brought
me out; and I was thinking, too, of the girls that are
going to America in the morning, and that made me
restless.

(MARTIN *and* CORNELIUS *look significantly at each
other.*)

MARTIN DOURAS : And did you see Matt, Ellen?

14

ELLEN : He was in the field and I coming up; but I did not wait for him, as I don't want people to see us together. (*Restlessly*). I don't know how I can come into this house, for it's always like Murtagh Cosgar. There's nothing of Matt in it at all. If Matt would come away. There are little labourers' houses by the side of the road. Many's the farmer's son became a labourer for the sake of a woman he cared for.

CORNELIUS : And are you not thinking about the school at all, Ellen?

ELLEN : I'll hear about it some time, I suppose.

MARTIN DOURAS : You're right to take it that way, Ellen. School doesn't mean scholarship now. Many's the time I'm telling Cornelius that a man farming the land, with a few books on his shelf and a few books in his head, has more of the scholar's life about him than the young fellows who do be teaching in schools and teaching in colleges.

CORNELIUS : That's all very well, Father. School and scholarship isn't the one. But think of the word 'Constantinople'! I could leave off herding and digging every time I think on that word!

MARTIN DOURAS : Ah, it's a great word. A word like that would make you think for days. And there are many words like that.

ELLEN : It's not so much the long words that we've to learn and teach now. When will you be home, Father? Will Cornelius be with you?

MARTIN DOURAS : Ellen, I have news for you. There's a school in Leitrim that Father Bartley can let you have.

ELLEN : In Leitrim! Did you tell Matt about it?

MARTIN DOURAS : I did not.

(SALLY *is heard calling* "*Cornelius.*" CORNELIUS *goes to the door.*)

15

CORNELIUS : Here's Matt now. The benefit of the day to you, Matt.

> (*He stands aside to let* MATT *enter.* MATT COSGAR *is about twenty-eight. He is handsome and well-built. He is dressed in a trousers, shirt, and coat, and has a felt hat on.* CORNELIUS *goes out.*)

MATT (*going to* ELLEN) : You're welcome, Ellen. Good morrow, Martin. It's a great day for the purchase, Martin.

MARTIN DOURAS : A great day, indeed, thank God.

MATT : Ah, it's a great thing to feel the ownership of the land, Martin.

MARTIN DOURAS : I don't doubt but it is.

MATT : Look at the young apple-trees, Ellen. Walking up this morning, I felt as glad of them as a young man would be glad of the sweetheart he saw coming towards him.

ELLEN : Ay, there's great gladness and shine in the day.

MATT : It seems to trouble you.

ELLEN : It does trouble me.

MATT : Why?

ELLEN : Everything seems to be saying, " There's something here, there's something going."

MATT : Ay, a day like this often makes you feel that way. It's a great day for the purchase though. How many years ought we to offer, Ellen?

> (MARTIN *goes out. He sits on the bench outside.*)

ELLEN : Twenty years, I suppose—(*suddenly*) Matt!

MATT : What's is it, Ellen?

ELLEN : I have got an offer of a school in the County Leitrim.

MATT : I wish they'd wait, Ellen. I wish they'd wait till I had something to offer you.

ELLEN : I'm a long time waiting here, Matt.

MATT : Sure we're both young.

16

ELLEN : This is summer now. There will be autumn in a month or two. The year will have gone by without bringing me anything.

MATT : He'll be letting me have my own way soon, my father will.

ELLEN : Murtagh Cosgar never let a child of his have their own way.

MATT : When the land's bought out, he'll be easier to deal with.

ELLEN : When he owns the land, he'll never let a son of his marry a girl without land or fortune.

MATT : Ellen, Ellen, I'd lose house and land for you. Sure you know that, Ellen. My brothers and sisters took their freedom. They went from this house and away to the ends of the world. Maybe I don't differ from them so much. But I've put my work into the land, and I'm beginning to know the land. I won't lose it, Ellen. Neither will I lose you.

ELLEN : O, Matt, what's the land after all? Do you ever think of America? The streets, the shops, the throngs?

MATT : The land is better than that when you come to know it, Ellen.

ELLEN : Maybe it is.

MATT : I've set my heart on a new house. Ay and he'll build one when he knows my mind.

ELLEN : Do you think he'd build a new house for us, Matt? I could settle down if we were by ourselves. Maybe it's true that there are things stirring and we could begin a new life, even here.

MATT : We can, Ellen, we can. Hush! Father's without.
(MARTIN DOURAS *and* MURTAGH COSGAR *are heard exchanging greetings. Then* MURTAGH *comes in,* MARTIN *behind him.* MURTAGH COSGAR *is about sixty. He is a hard, strong man, seldom-spoken, but with a flow of words and some satirical power. He*

17

is still powerful, mentally and physically. He is clean-shaven, and wears a sleeved waistcoat, heavy boots, felt hat. He goes towards ELLEN.)

MURTAGH : Good-morrow to you. (*Turning to* MATT). When I get speaking to that Sally again, she'll remember what I say. Giving cabbage to the pigs, and all the bad potatoes in the house. And I had to get up in the clouds of the night to turn cows out of the young meadow. No thought, no care about me. Let you take the harness outside and put a thong where there's a strain in it.

(MURTAGH *goes to the fire.* MATT *goes to the harness rack.* MARTIN DOURAS *and* ELLEN *are at the door.*)

MARTIN DOURAS : Ellen, I'll have news for you when I see you again. I've made up my mind to that.

ELLEN : Are you going to the fair, Father?

MARTIN DOURAS : Ay, with Murtagh.

ELLEN : God be with you, Father. (*She goes out.*)

MARTIN DOURAS : What purchase are you thinking of offering, Murtagh?

MURTAGH COSGAR : Twenty years.

MARTIN DOURAS : It's fair enough. Oh, it's a great day for the country, no matter what our own troubles may be.

(MATT *has taken down the harness. He takes some of it up and goes out.*)

MURTAGH COSGAR (*with some contempt*) : It's a pity you haven't a share in the day after all.

MARTIN DOURAS : Ay, it's a pity indeed.

(MURTAGH *goes to the door.*)

MURTAGH COSGAR (*with suppressed enthusiasm*) : From this day out we're planted in the soil.

MARTIN DOURAS : Ay, we're planted in the soil.

MURTAGH COSGAR : God, it's a great day.

(CORNELIUS *comes back.*)

18

CORNELIUS : This is a memorial occasion, Murtagh Cosgar, and I wish you the felicitations of it. I met the delegates and I coming in, and I put myself at the head of them. It's the day of the redemption, Murtagh Cosgar. (MURTAGH, *without speaking, goes up to the room* L.)

CORNELIUS : He's gone up to get the papers. Father, we must give the men understanding for this business. They must demand the mineral rights. Here they are. Men of Ballykillduff, I greet your entrance. (*Six men enter discussing.*)

FIRST MAN : We'll leave it to Murtagh Cosgar. Murtagh Cosgar isn't a grazier or a shopkeeper.

SECOND MAN : It's the graziers and shopkeepers that are putting a business head on this.

THIRD MAN : If we're all on the one offer, we can settle it at the lawyer's.

FOURTH MAN : Sure it's settled for twenty years on the first-term rents.

FIFTH MAN : There are some here that would let it go as high as twenty-three.

SIXTH MAN : What does Murtagh Cosgar say?

SOME OF THE MEN : We'll take the word from him.

MARTIN DOURAS : He mentioned twenty years.

SECOND MAN : Not as a limit, surely?

OTHER MEN : We're not for any higher offer.

SECOND MAN : Well, men, this is all I have to say. If you can get it for twenty, take it, and my blessing with it. But I want to be dealing with the Government, and not with landlords and agents. To have a straight bargain between myself and the Government, I'd put it up to twenty-three, ay, up to twenty-five years' purchase.

THIRD MAN : More power to you, Councillor. There's some sense in that.

19

SIXTH MAN : I'm with the Councillor.

FIRST MAN : It's all very well for graziers and shopkeepers to talk, but what about the small farmer?

FOURTH MAN : The small farmer. That's the man that goes under.

FIFTH MAN (*knocking at the table*) : Murtagh Cosgar! Murtagh Cosgar!

CORNELIUS : I tell you, men, that Murtagh Cosgar is in agreement with myself. Twenty years, I say, first term, no more. Let my father speak.

MARTIN DOURAS : There's a great deal to be said on both sides, men.

FIRST MAN : Here's Murtagh now.

MURTAGH COSGAR : Twenty years, first term, that's what I agreed to.

SECOND MAN : And if they don't rise to that, Murtagh?

MURTAGH COSGAR : Let them wait. We can wait. I won't be going with you, men. I had a few words with the agent about the turbary this morning, and maybe you're better without me.

FIRST MAN : All right, Murtagh. We can wait.

FOURTH MAN : We know our own power now.

FIFTH MAN : Come on, men.

MURTAGH COSGAR : If they don't rise to it, bide a while. We can make a new offer.

SECOND MAN : We want to be settled by the Fall.

THIRD MAN : The Councillor is right. We must be settled by the Fall.

SIXTH MAN : A man who's a farmer only has little sense for a business like this.

SECOND MAN : We'll make the offer, Murtagh Cosgar, and bide a while. But we must be settled this side of the Fall.

SIXTH MAN : We'll offer twenty years first term.

MURTAGH COSGAR : Do, and God speed you.

CORNELIUS (*to the men going out*) : I told you Murtagh
    Cosgar and myself are on the one offer. And Murtagh
    is right again when he says that you can bide your
    time. But make sure of the mineral rights, men;
    make sure of the mineral rights.

(*The men go out;* CORNELIUS *follows them.*)

MURTAGH COSGAR : Musha, but that's a well-discoursed
    lad. It must be great to hear the two of you at it.

MARTIN DOURAS : God be good to Cornelius. There's
    little of the world's harm in the boy.

MURTAGH COSGAR : He and my Sally would make a great
    match of it. She's a bright one, too.

MARTIN DOURAS : Murtagh Cosgar, have you no feeling
    for your own flesh and blood?

MARTIN COSGAR : Too much feeling, maybe. (*He stands
    at the door in silence.*) (*With sudden enthusiasm.*) Ah,
    but that's the sight to fill one's heart. Lands ploughed
    and spread. And all our own; all our own.

MARTIN DOURAS : All our own, ay. But we made a hard
    fight for them.

MURTAGH COSGAR : Ay.

MARTIN DOURAS : Them that come after us will never see
    them as we're seeing them now.

MURTAGH COSGAR (*turning round*) : Them that come after
    us. Isn't that a great thought, Martin Douras, and
    isn't it a great thing that we're able to pass this land
    on to them, and it redeemed for ever? Ay, and their
    manhood spared the shame that our manhood knew.
    Standing in the rain with our hats off to let a landlord
    —ay, or a landlord's dog-boy—pass the way!

MARTIN DOURAS (*mournfully*) : May it be our own genera-
    tion that will be in it. Ay, but the young are going
    fast; the young are going fast.

MURTAGH COSGAR (*sternly*) : Some of them are no loss.

21

MARTIN DOURAS : Your own children went, Murtagh Cosgar.

MURTAGH COSGAR : I never think of them. When they went from my control they went from me altogether. There's the more for Matt.

MARTIN DOURAS (*moistening his mouth, and beginning very nervously*) : Ay, Matt. Matt's a good lad.

MURTAGH COSGAR : There's little fear of him leaving now.

MARTIN DOURAS (*nervously*) : Maybe, maybe. But, mind you, Murtagh Cosgar, there are things—little things, mind you. Leastways, what we call little things. And, after all, who are we to judge whether a thing—

MURTAGH COSGAR : Is there anything on your mind, Martin Douras?

MARTIN DOURAS (*hurriedly*) : No; oh, no. I was thinking —I was thinking, maybe you'd give me a lift towards Arvach, if you'd be going that way this night.

MURTAGH COSGAR : Ay, why not?

MARTIN DOURAS : And we could talk about the land, and about Matt, too. Wouldn't it be a heartbreak if any of our children went—because of a thing we might—

MURTAGH COSGAR : What have you to say about Matt?

MARTIN DOURAS (*stammering*) : Nothing, except in a— in what you might call a general way. There's many a young man left house and land for the sake of some woman, Murtagh Cosgar.

MURTAGH COSGAR : There's many a fool did it.

MARTIN DOURAS (*going to door*) : Ay, maybe; maybe. I'll be going now, Murtagh.

MURTAGH COSGAR : Stop! (*he clutches Martin*) : You know about Matt. What woman is he thinking of?

MARTIN DOURAS : We'll talk about it again, Murtagh. I said I'd be back.

MURTAGH COSGAR : We'll talk about it now. Who is she? What name has she?

MARTIN DOURAS (*breaking from him and speaking with sudden dignity*): It's a good name, Murtagh Cosgar; it's my own name.

MURTAGH COSGAR: Your daughter! Ellen! Your girl!

MARTIN DOURAS: Ay, a good name, and a good girl.

MURTAGH COSGAR: And do you think a son of mine would marry a daughter of yours?

MARTIN DOURAS: What great difference is between us, after all?

MURTAGH COSGAR: The daughter of a man who'd be sitting over his fire reading his paper, and the clouds above his potatoes, and the cows trampling his oats. (MARTIN *is beaten down*). Do you know me at all, Martin Douras? I came out of a little house by the roadway and built my house on a hill. I had many children. Coming home in the long evenings, or kneeling still when the prayers would be over, I'd have my dreams. A son in Aughnalee, a son in Bally-brian, a son in Dunmore, a son of mine with a shop, a son of mine saying Mass in Killnalee. And I have a living name—a name in flesh and blood.

MARTIN DOURAS: God help you, Murtagh Cosgar.

MURTAGH COSGAR: But I've a son still. It's not your daughter he'll be marrying. (*He strides to the door and calls* MATT.)

MARTIN DOURAS (*going to him*): Murtagh Cosgar—for God's sake—we're both old men, Murtagh Cosgar.

MURTAGH COSGAR: You've read many stories, Martin Douras, and you know many endings. You'll see an ending now, and it will be a strong ending, and a sudden ending.

(MATT *comes to the door, holding the harness in his arms.*)

MURTAGH COSGAR: You're wanted here.

MATT: I heard you call (*coming down*). So they're sticking to the twenty years.

MARTIN DOURAS (*eagerly*): Twenty years, Matt, and they'll get it for twenty. O, it's a great day for you both! Father and son, you come into a single inheritance. What the father wins the sons wields.

MURTAGH COSGAR: What the father wins, the son wastes.

MATT: What's the talk of father and son.

MARTIN DOURAS: They're the one flesh and blood. There's no more strife between them than between the right hand and the left hand.

MURTAGH COSGAR (*to* MATT): We were talking about you. We were fixing a match for you.

MATT (*startled, looking at* MARTIN DOURAS): Fixing a match for me?

MURTAGH COSGAR: Ay, Matt. Don't you think it's time to be making a match for you?

MATT (*going to the door*): Maybe it is. When you have chosen the woman, call. I'll be without.

MURTAGH COSGAR (*going to him*): We haven't chosen yet. But it won't be Martin Douras' daughter, anyhow.

MATT: Stop. You drove all your living children away, except Sally and myself. You think Sally and myself are the one sort.

MURTAGH COSGAR: Martin's daughter, Corney's sister. That's the girl for you!

MATT: We're not the one sort, I tell you. Martin Douras, isn't he a foolish old man that would drive all his children from him. What would his twenty years' purchase be to him then?

MURTAGH COSGAR: It wasn't for my children I worked. No, no; thank God; it wasn't for my children I worked. Go, if you will. I can be alone.

MARTIN DOURAS: O, Murtagh, Murtagh, sure you know you can't be alone. We're two old men, Murtagh.

MURTAGH COSGAR: He daren't go.

24

MATT : Because I'm the last of them he thinks he can dare me like that.

MURTAGH COSGAR : There was more of my blood in the others.

MATT : Do you say that?

MARTIN DOURAS : Don't say it again. For God's sake, don't say it again, Murtagh.

MURTAGH COSGAR : I do say it again. Them who dared to go had more of my blood in them!

MATT : Ah, you have put me to it now, and I'm glad, glad. A little house, a bit of land. Do you think they could keep me here?

MURTAGH COSGAR (*to* MARTIN DOURAS) : It's his own way he wants. I never had my own way. (*To* MATT). You're my last son. You're too young to know the hardship there was in rearing you.

MATT : Your last son; that won't keep me here. I'm the last of my name, but that won't keep me here. I leave you your lands, your twenty years' purchase. Murtagh Cosgar, Murtagh Cosgar! isn't that a great name, Martin Douras—a name that's well planted, a name for generations? Isn't he a lucky man that has a name for generations? (*He goes out*).

MURTAGH COSGAR : He can't go. How could he go and he the last of the name. Close the door I say.

MARTIN DOURAS : He'll go to Ellen, surely. We'll lose both of them. Murtagh Cosgar, God comfort you and me.

MURTAGH COSGAR : Ellen; who's Ellen? Ay, that daughter of yours. They're a nice pair, a nice pair. Close the door I say.

(MARTIN DOURAS *closes the door and comes down to* MURTAGH COSGAR.)

CURTAIN

ACT TWO

Interior of Martin Douras'. The entrance is at back left. There is a dresser against wall back; a table down from dresser; room doors right and left. The fireplace is below the room door right; there are stools and chairs about it. There is a little bookcase left of the dresser, and a mirror beside it. There are cups and saucers on table, and a tea-pot beside fire. It is afternoon still. ELLEN DOURAS is near the fire reading. CORNELIUS comes in slowly.

CORNELIUS : I left the men down the road a bit. We ought to take great pride out of this day, Ellen. Father did more than any of them to bring it about.

ELLEN : He suffered more than any of them. And it's little we'll get out of the day.

CORNELIUS : It's a great thing to have prophesied it, even. We'll be here to see a great change.

ELLEN : There will be no change to make things better!

CORNELIUS : Will you be taking that school, Ellen?

ELLEN : I'll wait a while.

(SALLY *coming in; she is hurried.*)

SALLY (*breathlessly*) : Oh, God save you, Cornelius. Tell me, is my father gone? I dread going back and he there! It was all over that baste of a sow that has kept me slaving all through the spring till I don't know whether greens or potatoes is the fittest for her!

CORNELIUS : He didn't go, Sally. I went down a bit of the road myself with the men.

SALLY : Oh, God help me! And I'll have to be going back to boil meal for her now. How are you, Ellen? (*She goes to* ELLEN.)

ELLEN : Sit down for a while, Sally; it's a long time since I was speaking to you. (SALLY *sits down beside* ELLEN.)

26

CORNELIUS : I'll leave this paper where they won't be looking for pipe-lights. There are things in that paper I'd like to be saying. (*He takes a newspaper out of his pocket and goes to room R.*)

ELLEN (*to SALLY, who has been watching CORNELIUS*) : Tell me, Sally, are they always that busy in your house? Is your father as harsh as they say?

SALLY : Father 'ud keep us all working. He's a powerful great man.

ELLEN : Matt will be bringing a wife into the house soon from all I hear. How would your father treat her?

SALLY : Oh, he'd have his way, and she'd have her way, I suppose.

ELLEN : And do you think your father will let him marry?

SALLY : Sure he must if the boy likes.

ELLEN : What would he say if Matt married a girl without a fortune?

SALLY : In my mother's country there are lots of girls with fortunes that Matt could have.

ELLEN : Supposing he wanted a girl that had no fortune?

SALLY : Oh, I suppose, father would give in in the end. It wouldn't be clay against flint when Matt and father would be to it.

ELLEN : You're a good girl, Sally. If I was Matt's wife, do you think you'd be fond of me?

SALLY : I'd like you as well as another, Ellen.

(CORNELIUS *comes down from room.*)

CORNELIUS : I suppose they'll be here soon.

ELLEN : I have tea ready for them.

SALLY : Who's coming at all?

CORNELIUS : Some of the boys and girls that are for America. They are going to Gilroy's to-night, and are leaving from that in the morning. They are coming in to see Ellen on their way down.

27

SALLY : There are a good many going this flight. The land never troubles them in America, and they can wear fine clothes, and be as free as the larks over the bogs. It's a wonder you never thought of going, Ellen.

ELLEN : Father wouldn't like me to be far from him, and so I went in for the school instead.

SALLY : And now you've got a fine boy like Matt. It was lucky for you to be staying here.

ELLEN : Hush, Sally.

SALLY : Oh, I knew all about it before you talked to me at all. Matt always goes to the place where he thinks you'd be.

ELLEN (*rising*) : I'll be in the room when the girls come, Cornelius.

(*She goes into room L.*)

SALLY (*going to* CORNELIUS) : God help us, but she's the silent creature. Isn't it a wonder she's not filled with talk of him after seeing him to-day? But Ellen's right. We shouldn't be talking about men, nor thinking about them either; and that's the way to keep them on our hands in the long run. I'll be going myself.

(*She goes towards door.*)

CORNELIUS (*going to her*) : Don't be minding Ellen at all, Sally.

SALLY : Well, as high as she is, and as mighty as she is, she came into this house to see Matt. God between us and harm, Cornelius, maybe they'll be saying I came into your house to see you.

CORNELIUS : Who'll know you came at all? And what isn't seen won't be spoken of.

SALLY : Would you like me to stay, Cornelius?

CORNELIUS : Ay, I would.

SALLY : Divil mind the sow. (*They sit down together.*)

SALLY (*after a pause*) : Would you like me to knit you a pair of socks, Cornelius?

28

CORNELIUS : Oh, I would, Sally; I'd love to wear them.

SALLY : I'll knit them. We'll be getting rid of the sow to-night, maybe, and I'll have time after that.

CORNELIUS : And you come along the road when I'm herding. I don't want to be going near your father's house.

SALLY : O Cornelius, it won't be lucky for us when father hears about Ellen and Matt.

CORNELIUS : That's true. No man sees his house afire but looks to his rick.

SALLY : Come down a bit of the road with me, Cornelius. The sow will be grunting and grunting, reminding father that I'm away. Och, a minute ago I was as contented as if there was no land or pigs, or harsh words to trouble one. (*She goes to the door*). The boys and girls for America are coming here.

CORNELIUS : Give me your hands to hold, Sally. (*She gives him her hands.*) We are as young as any of them after all.

(*They hold each other's hands, then stand apart.*)

SALLY : It's a fine time for them to be going when the leaves are opening on the trees.

(*Three boys and three girls enter. They are dressed for going away.*)

SALLY : God save you, girls. Good-bye, Cornelius. I'll have to run like a redshank. (SALLY *goes out.*)

CORNELIUS : I'll call Ellen down to you. (*He goes to the room door and calls.*) I'm going herding myself. Herding is pleasant when you have thoughts with you. (*He takes up the rod and goes out.*)

(*The girls begin whispering, then chattering.*)

FIRST GIRL : Sure I know. Every night I'm dreaming of the sea and the great towns. Streets and streets of houses, and every street as crowded as the road outside the chapel when the people do be coming from Mass.

29

FIRST BOY : I could watch the crowd in the street; I would think it better than any sight I ever knew.

SECOND GIRL : And the shops and the great houses.

SECOND BOY : There's no stir here. There's no fine clothes, nor fine manners, nor fine things to be seen.

THIRD BOY : There's no money. One could never get a shilling together here. In America there's money to have and to spend and to send home.

THIRD GIRL : Every girl gets married in America. (ELLEN *comes down.*)

ELLEN : I'm glad you came. I have tea ready for you. I can't go to Gilroy's to-night.

(*Some come to the table and some remain near the door.*)

A GIRL (*at table, to* ELLEN) : They say that a turf fire like that will seem very strange to us after America. Bridget wondered at it when she came back. "Do civilized people really cook at the like of them?" she said.

A BOY : It's the little houses with only three rooms in them that will seem strange. I'm beginning to wonder myself at their thatch and their mud walls.

ANOTHER GIRL : Houses in bogs and fields. It was a heart-break trying to keep them as we'd like to keep them.

A GIRL (*at door*) : Ah, but I'll never forget Gortan and the little road to Aughnalee.

ANOTHER GIRL : I think I'll be lonesome for a long time. I'll be thinking of my brothers and sisters. I nursed and minded all the little ones.

FIRST BOY : A girl like you, Ellen, is foolish to be staying here.

SECOND BOY : She'll be coming in the Fall. We'll be glad to see you, Ellen.

ELLEN : I have no friends in America.

FIRST GIRL : I have no friends there, either. But I'll get on. You could get on better than any of us, Ellen.

SECOND GIRL : She's waiting for her school. It will be a little place by the side of a bog.

THIRD GIRL (*going to* ELLEN) : There would be little change in that. And isn't it a life altogether different from this life that we have been longing for? To be doing other work, and to be meeting strange people. And instead of bare roads, and market-towns, to be seeing streets, and crowds, and theatres.

ELLEN (*passionately*) : O what do you know about streets and theatres? You have only heard of them. They are finer than anything you could say. They are finer than anything you could think of after a story, when you'd be young.

A GIRL : You'll be going after all, Ellen.

ELLEN : I won't be going.

FIRST GIRL : Well, maybe you'll be down at Gilroy's. We must go now.

(*They rise,* ELLEN *goes to the door with the girls, and they part.*)

ELLEN : Theatres! What do they know of theatres? And it's their like will be enjoying them.

(SALLY *comes back. She is more hurried than before.*)

SALLY : Ellen! Ellen! I have wonders to tell. Where is Cornelius, at all? He's never here when you have wonders to tell.

ELLEN : What have you to tell?

SALLY : Oh, I don't know how I'll get it all out! Matt and father had an odious falling out, and it was about you. Matt's going to America; and he's to bring you with him. And Cornelius was saying that if father found out about yourself and Matt——

ELLEN : Sally, Sally, take breath, and tell it.

SALLY : Matt is going to America, like the others, and he's taking you with him.

ELLEN : Sally, Sally, is it the truth you're telling?

31

SALLY : It is the truth. Honest as day, it is the truth.

ELLEN : And I thought I'd be content with a new house. Now we can go away together. I can see what I longed to see. I have a chance of knowing what is in me. (*She takes* SALLY's *hands.*) It's great news you've brought me. No one ever brought me such news before. Take this little cross. You won't have a chance of getting fond of me after all. (*She wears a cross at her throat; she breaks the string, and gives it to* SALLY.)

SALLY : I don't know why I was so fervent to tell you. There's the stool before me that myself and Cornelius were sitting on, and he saying——(*she goes to the door*). Here's Matt! Now we'll hear all about it.

ELLEN : So soon, so soon. (*She goes to the mirror. After a pause, turning to* SALLY.) Go down the road a bit, when he comes in. Sally, you have a simple mind; you might be saying a prayer that it will be for the best.

SALLY (*going to the door muttering*) : Go down the road a bit! 'Deed and I will not till I know the whole ins and outs of it. Sure I'm as much concerned in it as herself! " No man sees his house afire but watches his rick," Cornelius was saying. Ah, there's few of them could think of as fine a thing as that. (MATT *comes in.*)

MATT : Well, Sally, were you home lately?

SALLY : I was——leastways as far as the door. Father and oul' Martin were discoorsing.

MATT : I've given them something to discoorse about. Maybe you'll be treated better from this day, Sally.

SALLY : O Matt, I'm sorry. (*She goes out.*)

MATT (*going to* ELLEN) : It happened at last, Ellen; the height of the quarrel came.

ELLEN : It was bound to come. I knew it would come, Matt.

MATT : He was a foolish man to put shame on me after all I did for the land.

32

ELLEN : You had too much thought for the land.

MATT : I had in troth. The others went when there was less to be done. They could not stand him. Even the girls stole away.

ELLEN : There was the high spirit in the whole of you.

MATT : I showed it to him. " Stop," said I; " no more, or I fling lands and house and everything aside."

ELLEN : You said that.

MATT : Ay. " Your other children went for less," said I; " do you think there's no blood in me at all ?"

ELLEN : What happened then?

MATT : " I'm your last son," I said; " keep your land and your twenty years' purchase. I'm with the others; and it's poor your land will leave you, and you without a son to bring down your name. A bit of land, a house," said I; " do you think these will keep me here?"

ELLEN : I knew they could not keep you here, Matt. You have broken from them at last; and now the world is before us. Think of all that is before us——the sea, and the ships, the strange life, and the great cities.

MATT : Ay——there before us——if we like.

ELLEN : Surely we like.

MATT : I was always shy of crowds. I'm simple, after all, Ellen, and have no thought beyond the land.

ELLEN : You said that house and land could not keep you. You told him you were going as your brothers went.

MATT : And I felt I was going. I frightened him. He'll be glad to see me back. It will be long before he treats me that way again.

ELLEN (*suddenly*) : MATT!

MATT : What is it, Ellen?

ELLEN : I don't know——I was upset——thinking of the quarrel. (*Putting her hands on his shoulders.*) My poor Matt. It was about me you quarrelled.

33

MATT : Ay, he spoke against you. I couldn't put up with that.

ELLEN : He does not know your high spirit. He does not know your strength.

MATT : I had too much thought for the land.

ELLEN : You had. Have thought for me now. There is no one in fair or market but would notice me. I was never a favourite. I lived to myself. I did not give my love about. You have never offered me anything. You can offer me the sights of great towns, and the fine manners, and the fine life.

MATT : Ellen! (*He draws a little away.*) It's not me that could offer the like of that. I never had anything to my hand but a spade.

ELLEN : Your brothers—think of them.

MATT : They all left someone behind them. I am the last of my name.

ELLEN : Why should that keep you back?

MATT : His name is something to a man. Could you hear of your own name melting away without unease? And you are a woman. A man feels it more.

ELLEN : I do not understand men. Will you go back to your father's house after he shaming you out of it?

MATT : He'll be glad to see me back. He'll never cast it up to me that I went.

ELLEN : Matt, your father said words against me. Will you go to him and take his hand after that?

MATT : It was little he said against you. It was against your father he spoke.

ELLEN (*sinking down on a chair, and putting her hands before her face*) : My God! After all my waiting, you talk like that.

MATT (*going to her*) : Ellen, Ellen, tell me what I can do for you? There's land and houses to be had here. Father will let me have my own way after this.

34

ELLEN : (*rising, with anger*). What does it matter to me whether he lets you have your own way or not? Do you think I could go into a farmer's house?

MATT : Ellen!

ELLEN : It's a bad hand I'd make of a farmer's house. I'm not the sort to be in one. I'm not like Sally.

MATT (*getting angry*) : Don't be talking that way, Ellen Douras.

ELLEN (*with greater vehemence*) : I must be talking like this. If you take me, you will have to go from your father's house. I always knew it. You ought to know it now, Matt Cosgar.

MATT : You didn't know it always. And you have let someone come between us when you talk like that.

ELLEN : I'm not one to be listening to what people say about you. Nor do I be talking in the markets about you.

MATT : I suppose not. You wouldn't have people think you gave any thought to me. I'm not good enough for you. The people you know are better.

ELLEN : You are foolish to be talking like that. You are foolish, I say.

MATT : I know I am foolish. Fit only to be working in drains and ditches in the winter. That's what you think.

ELLEN : Maybe it is.

MATT : Ellen Douras! Ellen Douras! A farmer's roof will be high enough for you some day.

ELLEN : May I never see the day. Go back, go back. Make it up with your father. Your father will be glad of a labourer.

MATT : Maybe you won't be glad if I go back; thinking on what you've said.

ELLEN : I said too much. We don't know each other at all. Go back. You have made your choice. (*She goes up to room L.*)

35

MATT : Very well, then. God above, am I to be treated everywhere like a heifer strayed into a patch of oats? Neither man nor woman will make me put up with this any longer. (*Going to door.*) When Ellen Douras wants me, she knows the place to send to. (*He stands at door. There is no sound from room. Going back he speaks loudly.*) I'll be waiting two days or three days to hear from Ellen Douras.

    (*There is no sound.* MATT *goes out. The room door is thrown open, and* ELLEN *comes down*).

ELLEN (*furiously*) : Two days or three days he'll wait for me. As if I'd go into any farmer's house. As if I'd get married at all, and the world before me. Two days or three days you'll wait. Maybe it's lonesome, weary years you'll be waiting, Matt Cosgar.

CURTAIN

ACT THREE

Interior of Murtagh Cosgar's. It is towards sunset. MURTAGH
COSGAR is standing before the door, looking out. MARTIN
DOURAS is sitting at the fire in an armchair.

MARTIN DOURAS : It's getting late, Murtagh Cosgar.

MURTAGH COSGAR : Ay, it's getting late.

MARTIN DOURAS : It's time for me to be going home.   I
    should be seeing Ellen. (*He rises*).

MURTAGH COSGAR : Stay where you are. (*Turning round.*)
    We're two old men, as you say. We should keep each
    other company for 'a bit.

MARTIN DOURAS : I should be going home to see Ellen.

MURTAGH COSGAR : If she's going, you can't stay here. Let
    you keep here.

MARTIN DOURAS : She'll be wondering what happened to
    me.

MURTAGH COSGAR : Divil a bit it will trouble her. You're
    going to the fair anyway?

MARTIN DOURAS : I have no heart to be going into a fair.

MURTAGH COSGAR : It's myself used to have the great heart.
    Driving in on my own side-car, and looking down on
    the crowd of them. It's twenty years since I took a
    sup of drink. Oh, we'll have drinking to-morrow
    that will soften the oul' skin of you. You'll be singing
    songs about the Trojans to charm every baste in the
    fair.

MARTIN DOURAS : We're both old men, Murtagh Cosgar.

MURTAGH COSGAR : And is there any reason in your
    scholarship why oul' men should be dry men? Answer
    me that!

MARTIN DOURAS : I won't answer you at all, Murtagh
    Cosgar. There's no use in talking to you.

MURTAGH COSGAR : Put it down on a piece of paper that oul' men should have light hearts when their care is gone from them. They should be like——

MARTIN DOURAS : There's nothing in the world like men with their rearing gone from them, and they old. (*Sally comes to the door; she enters stealthily.*)

MURTAGH COSGAR : Ha, here's one of the clutch home. Well, did you see that brother of yours?

SALLY : I did. He'll be home soon, Father.

MURTAGH COSGAR : What's that you say? Were you talking to him? Did he say he'd be home?

SALLY : I heard him say it, Father.

MARTIN DOURAS : God bless you for the news, Sally.

MURTAGH COSGAR : How could he go and he the last of them? Sure it would be against nature. Where did you see him, Sally?

SALLY : At Martin Douras's, Father.

MURTAGH COSGAR : It's that Ellen Douras that's putting him up to all this. Don't you be said by her, Sally.

SALLY : No, Father.

MURTAGH COSGAR : You're a good girl, and if you haven't wit, you have sense. He'll be home soon, did you say?

SALLY : He was coming home. He went round the long way, I'm thinking. Ellen Douras was vexed with him, Father. She isn't going either, Matt says, but I'm thinking that you might as well try to keep a corncrake in the meadow for a whole winter, as to try to keep Ellen Douras in Aughnalee.

MURTAGH COSGAR : Make the place tidy for him to come into. He'll have no harsh words from me. (*He goes up to the room.*)

SALLY : Father's surely getting ould.

MARTIN DOURAS (*sitting down*) : He's gone up to rest himself, God help him. Sally, a stor, I'm that fluttered, I dread going into my own house.

38

SALLY : I'll get ready now, and let you have a good supper before you go to the fair.

MARTIN DOURAS : Sit down near me, and let me hear everything, Sally. Was it Matt that told you, or were you talking to Ellen herself?

SALLY : O, indeed, I had a talk with Ellen, but she won't give much of her mind away. It was Matt that was telling me. " Indeed she's not going," said he, " and a smart young fellow like myself thinking of her. Ellen is too full of notions." Here's Matt himself. Father won't have a word to say to him. He's getting mild as he's getting ould, and maybe it's a fortune he'll be leaving to myself.

(MATT *comes to the door. He enters.*)

MATT : Where is he? He's not gone to the fair so early?

SALLY : He's in the room.

MATT : Were you talking to him at all? Were you telling him you saw myself?

SALLY : I was telling him that you were coming back.

MATT : How did he take it?

SALLY : Very quiet. God help us all; I think father's losing his spirit.

MATT (*going to* MARTIN) : Well, you see I've come back, Martin.

MARTIN DOURAS : Ay, you're a good lad. I always said you were a good lad.

MATT : How did father take it, Martin?

MARTIN DOURAS : Quietly, quietly. You saw Ellen?

MATT : Ay, I saw Ellen. (*Gloomily*). She shouldn't talk the way she talks, Martin. What she said keeps coming into my mind, and I'm troubled. God knows I've trouble enough on my head.

MARTIN DOURAS (*eagerly*) : What did she say, Matt Cosgar?

MATT : It wasn't what she said. She has that school in her mind, I know.

MARTIN DOURAS : And is there anything to keep her here, Matt Cosgar?

MATT : I don't know that she thinks much of me now. We had a few words, but there's nothing in the world I would put above Ellen Douras.

MARTIN DOURAS : I should be going to her.

MATT : Wait a bit, and I'll be going with you. Wait a bit. Let us talk it over. She wouldn't go from you, and you so old.

MARTIN DOURAS : God forgive my age, if it would keep her here. Would I have my Ellen drawing turf, or minding a cow, or feeding pigs?

MATT : I'm fond of her, Martin. She couldn't go, and I so fond of her. What am I doing here? I should be making it up with her. What good will anything be if Ellen Douras goes? (*He turns to the door, then stops.*) I came to settle with him. I mustn't be running about like a frightened child.

> (*The room door opens, and* MURTAGH COSGAR *is seen.* SALLY *has hung a pot over the fire, and is cleaning the dishes at the dresser.*)

MURTAGH COSGAR (*at the room-door*) : Sally, it's time to be putting on the meal. If you have any cabbage left, put it through the meal. (*To* MATT). You put the thong in the harness?

MATT : I did. (*Pause*). Well, I've come back to you.

MURTAGH COSGAR : You're welcome. We were making ready for the fair.

MATT : I'll be going out again before nightfall.

MURTAGH COSGAR : I'll not be wanting you here, or at the fair.

MATT (*sullenly*) : There's no good talking to me like that.

MURTAGH COSGAR : You said, " I've come back," and I said, " you're welcome." You said, " I'm going out again," and I said, " I'll not be wanting you."

40

MATT : Father, have you no feeling for me at all?

MURTAGH COSGAR : Sure the wild raven on the tree has thought for her young.

MATT : Ay, but do you feel for me, and I standing here, trying to talk to you?

MURTAGH COSGAR : You're my son, and so I feel sorry for you; and you beginning to know your own foolishness. (*He turns to* SALLY). I'm not taking the pigs. Put a fresh bedding under them to-night.

SALLY : I will, Father.

MURTAGH COSGAR : Be up early, and let the cows along the road, or they'll be breaking into the young meadow.

SALLY : I'll do that, too.

MURTAGH COSGAR : Be sure to keep enough fresh milk for the young calf.

SALLY : I'll be sure to do it, Father.

> (*She goes out.* MARTIN *takes out his paper, and begins to read it again.*)

MATT (*turning on* MURTAGH) : Before I go out again there's something I want settled.

MURTAGH COSGAR : What is it you want?

MATT : Would you have me go, or would you have me stay?

MURTAGH COSGAR : Don't be talking of going or staying, and you the last of them.

MATT : But I will be talking of it. You must treat me differently if you want me to stay. You must treat me differently to the way you treat Sally.

MURTAGH COSGAR : You were always treated differently, Matt. In no house that ever I remember was there a boy treated as well as you were treated here.

MATT : The houses that you remember are different from the houses that are now. Will you have me go, or will you have me stay?

MURTAGH COSGAR : You're very threatening. I'd have you stay. For the sake of the name, I'd have you stay.

MATT : Let us take hands on it, then.

MURTAGH COSGAR : Wait, we'll see what you want first.

MATT : You have no feeling. I'd go out of this house, only I want to give you a chance.

MURTAGH COSGAR : Stop. We can have kindness in this. We needn't be beating each other down, like men at a fair.

MATT : We're not men at a fair. May God keep the kindness in our hearts.

     (MARTIN *rises*.)

MURTAGH COSGAR : Don't be going, Martin Douras.

MATT : Don't be going yet. I'll be with you, when you're going.

     (MARTIN *sits down*.)

MURTAGH COSGAR (*To* MATT) : You'll be getting married I suppose, if you stay?

MATT : Maybe I will.

MURTAGH COSGAR (*bitterly*) : In the houses that are now, the young marry where they have a mind to. It's their own business, they say.

MATT : Maybe it is their own business. I'm going to marry Ellen Douras, if she'll have me.

MURTAGH COSGAR : Ellen is a good girl, and clever, I'm told. But I would not have you deal before you go into the fair.

MATT : I'm going to marry Ellen Douras.

MURTAGH COSGAR : Her father is here, and we can settle it now. What fortune will you be giving Ellen, Martin? That £100 that was saved while you were in Maryborough gaol? (MARTIN *shakes his head*.)

MATT (*stubbornly*) : I'm going to marry Ellen Douras, with or without a fortune.

MURTAGH COSGAR : Boy, your father built this house. He got these lands together. He has a right to see that you and your generations are in the way of keeping them together.

MATT : I'll marry Ellen Douras, with or without a fortune.

MURTAGH COSGAR : Marry her, then. Marry Ellen Douras.

MATT : Now, Martin, we mustn't let an hour pass without going to her. (*He takes* MARTIN'S *arm, and they go to the door.*)

MURTAGH COSGAR : Marry Ellen Douras, I bid you. Break what I have built, scatter what I have put together. This is what all the young will be doing.

    (ELLEN DOURAS *comes to the door as* MATT *and* MARTIN *reach it.*)

MATT : Ellen! (*She shrinks back.*)

ELLEN : It's my father I came to speak to.

MURTAGH COSGAR (*Going to the door, and drawing the bolt from the half-door.*) : When you come to my house, Ellen Douras, you are welcome within.

    (ELLEN *comes in.*)

ELLEN : It's right that I should speak to you all. Matt Cosgar, I am going from here.

MATT : Ellen, Ellen, don't be saying that. Don't be thinking of the few words between us. It's all over now. Father agrees to us marrying. Speak, Father, and let her hear yourself say it.

ELLEN : I can't go into a farmer's house.

MATT : You said that out of passion. Don't keep your mind on it any longer.

ELLEN : It's true, it's true. I can't go into a farmer's house. This place is strange to me.

MATT : How can you talk like that? I'm always thinking of you.

ELLEN : I've stayed here long enough. I want my own way; I want to know the world.

MATT : If you go, how will I be living, day after day? The heart will be gone out of me.

MURTAGH COSGAR : You'll be owning the land, Matt Cosgar.

MATT (*passionately*) : I've worked on the land all my days. Don't talk to me about it now.

(ELLEN *goes to* MARTIN. MURTAGH *goes up to the door, and then turns and speaks.*)

MURTAGH COSGAR : Listen to me, Matt Cosgar; and you listen too, Ellen Douras. It's a new house you want maybe. This house was built for me and my generations; but I'll build a new house for you both. It's hard for a man to part with his land before the hour of death; and it's hard for a man to break his lands; but I'll break them, and give a share of land to you.

ELLEN : You were never friendly to me; but you have the high spirit, and you deserve a better daughter than I would make. The land and house you offer would be a drag on me. (*She goes to the door.*)

MATT : Ellen, what he offers is nothing, after all; but I care for you. Sure you won't go from me like that?

ELLEN : Oh, can't you let me go? I care for you as much as I care for anyone. But it's my freedom I want.

MATT : Then you're going surely?

ELLEN : I am. Good-bye.

(*She goes out,* MARTIN *follows her.* MATT *stands dazed.* MURTAGH *closes the door, then goes and takes* MATT'S *arm, and brings him down.*)

MURTAGH COSGAR : Be a man. We offered her everything, and she went. There's no knowing what the like of her wants. The men will be in soon, and we'll drink to the new ownership.

MATT : Oh, what's the good in talking about that now? If Ellen was here, we might be talking about it.

MURTAGH COSGAR : To-morrow you and me might go together. Ay, the bog behind the meadow is well drained by this, and we might put the plough over it. There will be a fine, deep soil in it, I'm thinking. Don't look that way, Matt, my son.

44

MATT : When I meet Ellen Douras again, it's not a farmer's house I'll be offering her, nor life in a countryplace.

MURTAGH COSGAR : No one could care for you as I care for you. I know the blood between us, and I know the thoughts I had as I saw each of you grow up.

(MATT *moves to the door.*)

MURTAGH COSGAR : Where are you going?

MATT : To see the boys that are going away.

MURTAGH COSGAR : Wait till the Fall and I'll give you money to go and come back. Farrell Kavanagh often goes to America. You could go with him.

MATT : I'll go by myself, unless Ellen Douras comes now. The creamery owes me money for the carting and I'll get it.

MURTAGH COSGAR : Then go. Good-bye to you, Matt Cosgar.

MATT : Good-bye to you. (*He goes out.* MURTAGH *stands, then moves about vaguely.*)

MURTAGH COSGAR : The floor swept, the hearth tidied. It's a queer end to it all. Twenty years I bid them offer. Twenty years, twenty years.

(MARTIN *comes back.*)

MURTAGH COSGAR : The men will be coming back.

MARTIN DOURAS : I suppose they will.

MURTAGH COSGAR : You're a queer fellow, Martin Douras. You went to gaol for some meeting.

MARTIN DOURAS : Ay.

MURTAGH COSGAR : Them was the stirring times. I can't help but think of you in gaol, and by yourself. What brings you back now?

MARTIN DOURAS : Ellen told me to go back. I should say something to Matt, I think.

MURTAGH COSGAR : He went out as you came in.

MARTIN DOURAS : I'll go in when the house is quiet. I'll have a few prayers to be saying this night.

MURTAGH COSGAR : I'm going to the fair.

MARTIN DOURAS : I won't be going to the fair.

MURTAGH COSGAR : Why won't you be going to the fair? Didn't you ask me for a lift? You'll be going with me.

MARTIN DOURAS : I won't be going, and don't be over-bearing me now, Murtagh Cosgar.

MURTAGH COSGAR : You will be going to the fair, if it was only to be showing that seemly face of yours. (*Going to the door, he calls* SALLY. *He turns to* MARTIN DOURAS). I've a daughter still, Martin Douras.

MARTIN DOURAS : You have, and I have a son.

MURTAGH COSGAR : What would you say to a match between them, Martin Douras?

MARTIN DOURAS : I have nothing to say against it.

MURTAGH COSGAR : Then a match it will be.

(SALLY *enters.*)

SALLY : If you fed that baste on honey, she'd turn on you. Cabbage I gave her and got into trouble for it, and now she's gone and trampled the bad potatoes till they're hardly worth the boiling. I'll put the bush in the gap when I'm going out again, Father.

MURTAGH COSGAR : Ay. Is that Cornelius Douras that's coming up the path?

SALLY : O faith it is. I'll get him to give me a hand with the trough.

(CORNELIUS *enters.*)

CORNELIUS : Well, Murtagh Cosgar, a great and memorial day is ended. May you live long to enjoy the fruits of it. Twenty years on the first term, and the land is ours and our children's. I met the men.

MURTAGH COSGAR : Ours and our children's, ay. We've been making a match between yourself and Sally.

CORNELIUS : Between me and Sally?

SALLY : Between Cornelius and myself?

46

CORNELIUS (*enthusiastically*) : And we're the ones for each other, Sally and me! (*Holding* SALLY's *hands*). Is it true that Matt's going to America, and that Ellen will wait for him for a year at the school? I met them together, and they told me that.

MURTAGH COSGAR : What they say is true, I'm sure. The land is yours and your children's.

MURTAGH COSGAR : Ay, shake hands on it now.

SALLY : O Cornelius.

CORNELIUS : Aren't they foolish to be going away like that, Father, and we at the mouth of the good times? The men will be coming in soon, and you might say a few words. (MARTIN *shakes his head*). Indeed you might, Father; they'll expect it of you. (MARTIN *shakes his head.* MURTAGH *and* SALLY *try to restrain hi*m.) " Men of Ballyhillduff," you might say, " Stay on the land, and you'll be saved body and soul; you'll be saved in the man and in the nation. The nation, men of Ballyhillduff, do you ever think of it at all? Do you ever think of the Irish nation that is waiting all this time to be born?"

(*He becomes more excited; he is seen to be struggling with words.*)

CURTAIN

FINIS

The Fiddler's House

A play in three acts

Characters

CONN HOURICAN (*a fiddler*)
MAIRE HOURICAN (*his daughter*)
ANNE HOURICAN (*a younger daughter*)
BRIAN McCONNELL (*a young farmer*)
JAMES MOYNIHAN (*a farmer's son*)
JUSTIN REILLY (*a student for the priesthood*)

The action passes in the Houricans' cottage
in the Irish Midlands.

Period: The end of the nineteenth century.

Scene: Interior of the Houricans' cottage.

ACT ONE

The entrance is back right; the half-door is closed and one can see across the cottage yard beyond which are fields. Left of entrance is a shelf; left centre is a window, un-expectedly high and wide for the size of the cottage; under it is a bench which contains a locker beneath; there is a room door left and a fire-place with a wide hearth with a chimney-piece above. On the right is a dresser; above it a room with some steps going up to it, and back, right of entrance is a rack on which men's coats hang. There is a table centre, chairs and stools; a pitcher by the dresser.

It is the afternoon of a harvest day. JAMES MOYNIHAN, a young man, who looks a little staid and self-satisfied, is finishing a meal at the table. ANNE HOURICAN has been attending him. She is pretty, self-contained, and quiet.

JAMES MOYNIHAN rises.

ANNE (*rising and moving to table*): You can't stay any longer, James?

JAMES (*with certain solemnity*): No, Anne. I told my father I'd be back while there was light, and I'm going back. (*He goes to the rack, takes his coat, and puts it on.* ANNE *moves to the dresser with dishes*). Come over to our house to-night, Anne. I'll be watching the other girls coming in, and thinking of yourself; there's none of them to match your grace and favour. My father wanted me to see a girl in Arvach. She has three hundred pounds besides what the priest, her uncle, will leave her. " Father," says I, " listen to me now. Haven't I always worked for you like a steady useful boy?" " You have," says he. " Did I ever ask you for anything unreasonable?" says I.

"No," says he. "Well then," says I, "don't ask me to do unreasonable things. I'm fond of Anne Hourican, and not another girl will I marry. What's money, after all?" says I. "There's gold on the whin bushes if you only knew it." And he had to leave it at that.

ANNE (*moving to back of table L.*): You always bring people around.

JAMES: The quiet, reasonable way is the way that people like.

ANNE: Still, with all, I'm shy of going into your house.

JAMES: Don't doubt but there'll be a welcome before you; come around with Maire.

> (ANNE *comes to him and puts her hands on his shoulders. She has graceful, birdlike movements.*)

ANNE: Maybe we won't have a chance of seeing each other after all.

> (JAMES *kisses her reverently.*)

JAMES: Sit down now, Anne, because there's something I want to show you. (*They go to settle and sit down.*) Do you ever see "The Shamrock"?

ANNE: Very seldom.

JAMES: There be good pieces in it sometimes. There's a poem of mine in it this week.

ANNE: Of yours, James? Printed, do you mean?

JAMES: Ay, printed. (*He takes a paper out of his pocket and opens it.*) It's a poem to yourself, though your name doesn't come into it. (*Gives paper.*) Let no one see it, Anne, at least not for the present. And now, good-bye. (*Goes to door.* ANNE *continues reading the verse eagerly. At the door* JAMES *turns and recites*):

> When the lights are failing, and the skies are paling,
>   And leaves are sailing a-down the air,
> O, it's then that love lifts my heart above,
>   My roving thoughts and my petty care;
> And though the gloom be like the tomb,

52

Where there's no room for my love and me,
    O, still I'll find you, and still I'll bind you,
        My wild sweet rose of Aughnalee!
That's the first stanza. Good-bye. (*He goes out.*)
            (ANNE *continues reading, then she leaves the paper
            down with a sigh.*)
ANNE : O, it's lovely! (*She takes the paper up again, rises and
    goes to the door. She remains looking out. Someone speaks
    to her.*) No, Brian, Maire's not back yet. Ay, I'll
    engage she'll give you a call when she does come back.
    (ANNE *turns back. She opens drawer in dresser and puts
    paper in. She begins to clear table, putting delf back on
    dresser. To herself, anxiously*) : I hope Maire won't
    forget to call at the mill.
            (*Room door right opens and* CONN HOURICAN *comes
            down. He is a man of about sixty, with clear-cut
            features, his face is clean-shaven, his expression,
            vehement. His dress is old-fashioned. He carries a
            stick and moves about restlessly.*)
ANNE : Had Maire any talk about going to the mill, Father?
CONN (*crossing to fireplace*) : I heard nothing about it.
ANNE (*crossing to dresser*) : I hope she'll mind of it. We
    must get the meal there, and not be going to the shop
    so often.
CONN : I suppose we must. (*He moves about restlessly.*)
ANNE : And I was thinking that one of us ought to go to
    Arvach on Tuesday, and get the things there.
            (CONN *has taken a cup of water. He goes to the fire.*)
CONN : The mean, odious creatures!
ANNE (*startled, turning from dresser*) : What are you think-
    ing of, Father?
CONN : That den of robbers. Well, well, I'm finished with
    them now; but I'm a proud man, and a passionate man,
    and I'll be even with them yet. (*He drinks from the
    cup.*)

53

ANNE : There's no comfort in going into rough places.

CONN : You know nothing at all about it. (*Drinks*). Were the men in yet?

ANNE : James Moynihan was here, because he had to go away early; but Brian McConnell is outside still. Father, you were home late two nights this week.

CONN : And is a man to have no life to himself? But sure you know nothing at all about it. I'm going out now to give Brian McConnell a hand.

ANNE : It's hardly worth while going out now.

CONN : There's still light enough to do a bit of mowing, and you ought to know that it isn't right to neglect the boy that's come to do a day's work with you. (*Going to door. Takes coat.*) Many's the day I put in with the scythe in Ireland, and in England too; I did more than stroll with the fiddle, and I saw more places than where fiddling brought me.

(BRIAN MCCONNELL *comes to the door.*)

I was just going out to you, Brian. I was telling the girl here that it's not right to neglect the boy that's giving you a day's work out of his own goodness.

BRIAN : I'm only coming in for a light.

CONN : As you're here now, rest yourself.

(BRIAN *comes in and goes over to hearth. He is dark and good-looking, and has something reckless in his look. He wears corduroy trousers, and a shirt loose at the neck.* CONN *stands at entrance, his back turned.*)

(BRIAN *lights his pipe with a coal. Beckons to* ANNE *who crosses to him.*)

BRIAN : When do you expect Maire back?

ANNE : She'll be here soon. She'll give you a call if you're outside.

BRIAN : How is it you couldn't keep James Moynihan?

54

ANNE : It's because you didn't say the good word for me. I must think. Be sure you praise me the next time you're working together.

BRIAN : Will you do as much for me?

ANNE : Indeed, I will, Brian. Myself and another are making a devotion to Saint Anthony.

BRIAN : And what would that be for?

ANNE (*taking up tablecloth*) : That the Saint might send us good comrades.

BRIAN : I thought it was Saint Joseph did that for the girls.

ANNE (*folding tablecloth*) : Sure we couldn't be asking the like from him. We couldn't talk to Saint Joseph that way. We want a nice young saint to be looking at. (*Crosses to dresser.*)

      (CONN *turns from door.*)

CONN (*bitterly*) : It'll be a poor season, Brian McConnell.

BRIAN : The season's not so bad after all.

CONN : God help them that are depending on the land and weather for the bit they put into their heads. It's no wonder that the people here are the sort they are, harassed, anxious people.

ANNE : The people here mind their own business, and they're a friendly people besides.

CONN : People that would leave the best fiddler at the fair and go and look at a bullock.

ANNE (*to* BRIAN) : He's not satisfied to have this shelter, Brian.

CONN (*to* BRIAN) : I'm saying, Brian, that her mother had this shelter, and she left it to go the roads with myself.

ANNE : That God may rest my mother. It's a pity she never lived to come back to the place. But we ought to be praising grandmother night and day, for leaving this place to Maire.

CONN : Your grandmother did that as she did everything else.

55

ANNE (*moving cups*) : Now, Brian, what would you do with a man would say the like ? (*She takes empty pail and goes outside.*)

CONN : It's a small blame to the girl for thinking something of the place; but I saw the time, Brian McConnell, when I could make more playing at one fair than working a whole season in this bit of a place.

BRIAN : Girls like the shelter, Conn.

CONN : Ay, but the roads for the fiddler. I'm five years settled here, and I come to be as well known as the begging ass, and there is as much thought about me. Fiddling, let me tell you isn't like a boy's whistling. It can't be kept up on nothing.

BRIAN : I understand that, Conn.

CONN : I'm getting that I can't stand the talk you hear in houses, wars and parliaments, and the devil knows what ramais.

BRIAN : There's still a welcome for the man of art, some-where.

CONN : That somewhere's getting further and further away, Brian.

BRIAN : Were you not in town last night?

CONN : I was not, Brian, God help me, I spent the night my lone.

BRIAN : There's Sligomen in the town.

CONN : Is there, now? It would be like oul' times to play for them.

(ANNE *comes in with turf and pail.*)

Anne, would you bring me down my spectacles? They're in the room, daughter.

(ANNE *leaves down turf and pail and goes to room.* CONN *turns to* BRIAN *eagerly.*)

I suppose the Sligomen will be in Flynn's.

BRIAN : They were there last night.

CONN : Listen, Brian, I've a reason for not going to Flynn's. Would you believe it, Brian, Flynn spoke to me about the few shillings I owe him?

BRIAN : That was shabby of him. He got a lot out of you in the way of playing.

CONN : It's just like them. Besides, Maire keeps us tight enough and I often have to take treats from the men. They're drovers, and rambling labourers and the like, though, as you say, they've the song and music, and the proper talk. Listen, Brian, could you leave a few shillings on the mantel-shelf for me?

BRIAN : To be sure I will, Conn. (*He puts some money on mantel-shelf and moves across to the door.*)

CONN (*with dignity*) : Thank you, Brian. There's few I'd let put me under a compliment, but I take it from you. (*He takes the money from the shelf.*) Maire, as I said, is a careful girl, but some of us must have our freedom. Besides, Brian, the bird that sings lone sings slow. The man of art must have his listeners. (*Going to room door.*) Anne, daughter, what's keeping you up there? Sure the spectacles were in my pocket the whole time, child. (*He goes to settle and sits.*) When I spoke against the people about here, I was leaving you out of it, Brian.

(ANNE *enters from room and goes to fire to put on turf.*)
(BRIAN *is still at the door.*)

ANNE : You'll be staying on in these parts now, won't you, Brian?

BRIAN : I won't be going away again. I made it up with my brothers.

ANNE : They use to say that a McConnell quarrel was a lasting quarrel.

BRIAN : Maybe we're working the bad blood out of us.

ANNE : Well, we'll want you back soon, Brian.

57

BRIAN : I'll be no longer than till Maire gives me the call. (*Exit*).

ANNE : Imagine that!

CONN (*in good humour*) : What, Auneen?

ANNE : Brian McConnell getting so quieted down! Making it up with his brothers, no less, when we all thought he was as wild as a hunter!

CONN : We only know what people said about the McConnells until Brian became friendly.

ANNE : There's a change in him, anyway. Maire used to be afeard of him.

CONN : Of Brian—afeard of him?

ANNE : She never told me she was, but I knew it from her. But it's all past and gone, whatever it was shook her about him. Well, we mustn't take another day from him. He's more used to his horses than he is to fields.

CONN : You can depend on me to finish the mowing. There's only a patch at the back to be done. (*Rising and going towards room.*) I'm going up now to go over an oul' tune I have.

ANNE : James Moynihan would come over and stack for us.

CONN : James Moynihan is a decent boy, too.

ANNE : You won't be going out to-night, Father?

CONN : Now, how's a man to know what he'll be doing?

ANNE : Ah, dear me! It leaves me very anxious.

CONN : I'll give you this advice, and it's proper advice to give to a girl thinking of marrying. (*Moves towards her.*) Never ask of your menkind where they're going. (*Places hand on Anne's.*)

ANNE : The like of that brings bad luck on a house.

CONN : You have too much dead knowledge, and the shut fist never caught a bird.

ANNE : I only wish you'd settle down.

CONN : Sure I am settled down.

ANNE : I can't speak to you, after all.

58

CONN (*going to her affectionately*) : You're a good girl, Anne, and he'll be lucky that gets you. And don't be grieving that you're not bringing James Moynihan a fortune. You're bringing him the decency of birth and rearing. You're like the lone pigeon I often think—the pet that doesn't fly, and keeps near the house.

ANNE : That's the way you always treat me, and I never can talk to you.

(MAIRE *is heard singing off.*)

CONN (*at window*) : Hush now, here's the other, your sister Maire. She's like the wild pigeon of the woods.

(*Suddenly the singing stops.* MAIRE HOURICAN *comes in* R.)

We were discoursing on affairs, Maire. We won't be bringing Brian McConnell here to-morrow; there's only the bit at the back to be mown, and I'll do that myself. (*He goes into the room* R.; *soon after the fiddle is heard.*)

(ANNE *goes to settle and takes up her knitting.* MAIRE *takes her shawl off and hangs it on rack.* MAIRE HOURICAN *is over twenty. She is tall, and has easy graceful movements; her features are fine and clear-cut, the nose is rather blunted, the mouth firm. Her gaze is direct and clear. She has heavy auburn hair, loose now, and falling.* MAIRE *comes down to the dresser, opens basket and takes some flowers from top. She arranges some of the flowers in a jar.*)

MAIRE : We'd have no right to take another day from Brian. And when there's no one here to-morrow, you and me could draw some of the turf.

ANNE : Your hair is loose, Maire.

(MAIRE *goes to the mirror and fixes her hair.*)

MAIRE : The wind blew it about me, and then I let it down. I came home by the long way, just to feel young again with my hair about me.

59

ANNE : And did you meet anyone?

MAIRE : Indeed I did. I met James Moynihan.

ANNE : James had to go early. They're building at his place.

MAIRE : Indeed they ought to let James build a house for himself.

ANNE : Some day they will, Maire.

MAIRE : But we must not let some day be a far day. (*Crossing to settle.*)

ANNE (*hesitatingly*) : I think I'll show you something.
   (ANNE *rises and goes to the dresser. She opens the drawer.* MAIRE *watches her.*)

MAIRE (*waiting*) : I made a good girl out of you, anyway.

ANNE : You wouldn't let me use stroller words when we were on the road. Do you mind of that?

MAIRE : I kept you to the mannerly ways. I have that to my credit.
   (ANNE *comes to* MAIRE *and shows her the verses.*)

ANNE : Read that, Maire. It was James that made it.

MAIRE : It's a song, I declare.

ANNE : No, Maire, it's a poem.

MAIRE : A poem? O, that's grand! (*She begins to read it eagerly.*)

ANNE : And, Maire——

MAIRE : Well?

ANNE : James says it's about me.

MAIRE : About you? O, I wish someone would put me into a song, or into a poem ; I suppose a poem would be best. You might ask James. No, I'll coax him myself. Ah, no I won't, Anne.

ANNE : Six verses he made ! No less ! Isn't he a great hand at poetry?

MAIRE : He must be very fond of you, and I thinking him so quiet.

ANNE (*happy*) : He has grand thoughts about me.

MAIRE : Well, you'll be seeing him to-night.

ANNE : I don't think I'll go out to-night. (*She crosses to hearth.*)

MAIRE : Sure Grace Moynihan asked us to go over.

ANNE : I'm shy of going into James'.

MAIRE : Anne, you're the only one of us that has any manners. Maybe you're right not to go.

ANNE : I'll stay here to-night. (*Sits on settle.*)

MAIRE : Then Brian and myself will go to Moynihan's.

ANNE : You'd get an indulgence, Maire, if you missed a dance.

MAIRE : Would it be so hard to get an indulgence? (*She goes to the dresser, takes the flowers and puts them in window.*) The house looks nice this evening. We'll keep Brian here for a while, and then we'll go to Moynihan's.

ANNE : Father will be going out to-night.

MAIRE (*turning suddenly from window*) : Will he?

ANNE : He will. I think I ought to stay in. Maire, father was in only a while before you the night before last and another night.

MAIRE : O and I thinking things were going so well with us. He's drinking again.

ANNE : He's going to Flynn's again.

MAIRE : Disgracing us again.

ANNE : I'll stay in to-night.

MAIRE : I'm tired of this. (*Going to R. of table.*)

ANNE : Don't say it that way, Maire.

MAIRE : What will people say to us now?

ANNE : I'll talk to him to-night.

MAIRE : No, you're going out—you're going to Moynihan's—you're going to see your sweetheart.

61

ANNE : I think you're becoming a stranger to us, Maire.
(*Fiddle ceases*).

MAIRE : You're going to Moynihan's to-night, and I'm
going, too. But I'm going to settle this first. Once and
for all I'm going to settle this.
(MAIRE *goes towards room, and, as she does so,* CONN
comes down, the fiddle in his hand.)

CONN : Were you listening to the tune I was playing? Ah,
that was a real oul' tune, if there was anyone that
knew it. Maire, my jewel, were you listening?

MAIRE : I heard you.

CONN (*coming down*) : It was a real oul' tune, and while I
was playing it a great scheme came into my head.
Now, listen to me, Maire; and you listen, too, Anne.
Both of you would like to see your father having
what's his due after all, honour and respect.

MAIRE : Both of us would like to see our father earn the
same.

CONN : I could earn the same, ay, and gold and silver cups
besides if I had the mind to earn them. (*He puts fiddle
on table and prepares to speak impressively.*) Let ye listen
to me now; I've a scheme to put before ye. When I
was going over the oul' tune, I remembered that I'd
heard of a Feis that's coming on soon, the Feis of
Ardagh. I'm thinking of going there. There will be
great prizes for someone; I don't doubt but I'd do at
Ardagh better than I did at the Feis of Granard, where
people as high as bishops were proud and glad to know
Conn Hourican, the fiddler.

ANNE : Father, you've a place to mind.

CONN : I'm tired of that kind of talk; sure I'm always
thinking of the place. Maire hasn't little notions.
What do you say to it, Maire, my girl?

MAIRE : What do I say? I say you're not a rambler now,
though indeed you behave like one.

62

CONN : You have something against me, Maire.

MAIRE : I have.

CONN : What has she against me, Anne?

MAIRE : All the promises you broke.

CONN : You were listening to what the town is saying.

MAIRE : What does the town know? Does it know that you stripped us of stock and crop the year after we came here? Does it know that Anne and myself, two girls of the roads, had to struggle ever since to keep a shelter?

CONN (*bitterly*) : It knows that.

MAIRE : It couldn't help but know it, maybe. But does it know all the promises you made and broke?

CONN (*angrily*) : Hush now; I'll hear no more. I went my own way always, and I'll go my own way always. (*He goes to door, and remains with his back turned.*)

  (MAIRE *goes to* ANNE.)

MAIRE (*raising her voice*) : Ay, he'll go his own way always. What was the good of working and saving here? (*She goes to hearth stool.*)

ANNE : Be quiet with him.

MAIRE : He'll go his own way always, and it's foolish of us to be fretting for him night and day. (*She sits on stool and puts her hands across her face.*)

CONN (*turning his head*) : Fretting for me. It was too easy that I reared you.

ANNE : God help Maire. She kept the house together at the worst, and she is always fretting for us.

CONN : I'm oul' enough to mind myself. Let her remember that.

ANNE : It's you that ought to remember that.

  (CONN *goes to* MAIRE.)

CONN : Did I ever give the harsh word to you, child? (*No answer*). There, there; I never could see tears in a woman's eyes; there, there, colleen. I'm an oul' man; I won't be a trouble to you long.

MAIRE : Why need you play in Flynn's? You're as good as any that goes there.

CONN : I know that. I'm disgusted with Flynn. May hell loosen his knees for him! I'll go in and throw his money on the counter.

MAIRE : Some one else can do that. (*Rises and moves to* CONN.) Promise me you won't go near the place.

CONN : You'll have me promise. I promise.

MAIRE : Take this in your hand and promise. It's a medal that belonged to mother. (*She takes the medal from her neck.*)

CONN (*taking the medal*) : I'm disgusted with Flynn. I promise you, Maire.

MAIRE : Now you're honour and respect. (*Moving upstage.*)

CONN : And what about Ardagh, Maire?

MAIRE : Sure, you're not the rambling fiddler any more.

CONN : That would be good rambling. I can see the trees making shadows across the roads.

MAIRE : We'll talk about it again.

ANNE : Brian McConnell will be coming in now.

CONN : I'm going out to Brian McConnell. (*He goes to the door.*)

ANNE : Tell Brian to come in now.

(CONN *goes out. There is a pause.* MAIRE *hums a tune as she goes to the mirror.*)

MAIRE : Am I looking well to-day?

ANNE (*rather distantly*) : You're looking your best, I think. (*Rising*). Maire, I didn't like the way you talked to father.

MAIRE (*petulantly*) : What have you against it?

ANNE : You're becoming a stranger to us, Maire.

MAIRE (*as an apology*) : I'm out often, I know, but I think as much as ever of the house, and about you and father. You know we couldn't let him go to the Feis at Ardagh. We couldn't let him go off like a rambling fiddler.

64

ANNE : We couldn't let him go off by himself.

MAIRE : You're going to Moynihan's. (*Cross to door.*)

ANNE : Maybe I'll go.

MAIRE (*looking out doorway*) : Anne, honey, do something for me.

ANNE (*rising and going to her*) : What will I do?

MAIRE : You'll meet father coming up with Brian, and take him away.

ANNE : And will you tell me everything to-night? (*Hugs* MAIRE).

> (ANNE *goes out.* MAIRE *goes to lamp and lights it.* BRIAN MCCONNELL *comes in.*)

BRIAN : We didn't finish to-day. I'll come in to-morrow and finish.

MAIRE : O no, Brian, we won't take another day from you.

BRIAN : Well, what's a day after all? Many's the day and night I put in thinking on you. (*He sits on settle.*)

MAIRE : Did you do what I asked you?

BRIAN : I did. I made it up with them.

MAIRE : O, Brian, I'm well-pleased to hear that! (*She sits beside him.*)

BRIAN : It was never my way before to make it up with people that were against me.

MAIRE : Indeed they say that about Brian McConnell. Do you know, Brian, I was afraid of you one time?

BRIAN : And did I give you any reason to be?

MAIRE : I didn't know at all at that time. When I do know you my thoughts about you are different. Tell me what happened when you went to make it up with your brothers?

BRIAN : Hugh came to the door. "What destruction are you bringing here?" he said . . . That's the way we made it up. And Rose said . . .

MAIRE : Was Rose, your sister, there, Brian?

BRIAN : She was.

MAIRE : Rose was as well-pleased as myself—I'm sure of that.

BRIAN : But that man, Canavan, was with her, and I've reason to have a grudge against him.

MAIRE : I'm fond of Rose. Did you ever hear people say we were like each other, Rose and myself?

BRIAN : I think you are like each other.

MAIRE : Well, you wouldn't be hard on Rose, I know. That's settled. I think you could settle anything, Brian.

BRIAN : That's according as you'd ask me, Maire.

MAIRE : Maybe I'll ask you to settle lots of things. Oh, Brian, I wonder if you could settle something for us!

BRIAN : What is it, Maire?

MAIRE : It's my father. He wants to be rambling again. He wants to be going to some Feis.

BRIAN (taking her hand) : Sure, let him go.

MAIRE : I couldn't, Brian. Couldn't you help us? Couldn't you keep father's mind on the right things?

BRIAN : Sure let the fiddler go on the roads.

MAIRE : You might stay here this evening with ourselves. Father would be glad to talk with you.

(BRIAN puts his arm around her. There is resistance in her voice.)

MAIRE : Stay here with us, and let all that go by.

BRIAN : Hugh will be there with that woman that brought him the big fortune; and I want you to take the shine out of her.

MAIRE (rising and crossing in front of Brian) : I was out often lately. You know that, Brian.

BRIAN (rising and going to her) : But this night above all you must be with me.

MAIRE (turning to him impulsively) : Stay here and I'll be as nice to you as if we were in another house. (He takes her to him forcefully and kisses her.)

66

If you knew me at all, Brian McConnell, that's not the way you'd treat me. (*She moves towards fire.*)

BRIAN : Are you not coming out with me?

MAIRE : You must leave me to myself now.

(CONN *comes in.*)

Is Anne with you, Father?

CONN : She's gathering posies or something like that. Brian, did you hear about the Feis at Ardagh?

MAIRE (*with vehemence*) : Oh, what's the good of talking about that? You can't go.

CONN : Can't go, did you say, girl?

MAIRE : Oh, how could you go?

CONN : Is that the way? Well, God help us. Give me that fiddle till I leave it up. (*He takes the fiddle off table, and turns to go.*)

MAIRE : Father, let me be with you to-night; oh, I'm sorry if I vexed you. (*No reply.*) Well, stay with Brian McConnell; I'm going out to Anne. (*Exit.*)

BRIAN : Are you coming, Conn? I'm off.

CONN : Where to, man?

BRIAN : To Flynn's. (*He goes to rack and puts on his coat.*)

CONN (*crossing to fire*) : I can't be going, I'm sorry to say.

BRIAN : I'm going anyway. It's a great thing to be in the company of men.

CONN : Ay, in troth. Women, Brian, leave the heart very lonesome. (*He sits by the fire.*)

BRIAN (*masterfully*) : Why can't you come out? I thought you were going to-night.

CONN : I can't, Brian, and that reminds me. Give these few shillings to Flynn for me. I'll owe them to you still.

BRIAN : I'm not going to be bothered by the like. Why can't you come?

CONN : I promised Maire.

(BRIAN *strides away. He turns, comes back deliberately and leans on back of settle.*)

67

BRIAN : They'll be all looking out for you at Flynn's.

CONN : Well, the next time they see me they may respect me.

BRIAN : Some of the boys will take it very unkindly.

CONN : They're decent enough fellows, some of them.

BRIAN : And above all nights they'll be watching out for you this night on account of the Sligomen.

CONN : They're decent enough fellows, as I said, and I'll be sorry to disappoint them.

BRIAN : The Sligomen will have great stories about Shawn Heffernan.

CONN : Shawn Heffernan! Is that impostor still alive?

BRIAN : He is, and for fiddling these Sligomen think there's not the like of him in the whole of Ireland.

CONN : God help them if that's all they know. We played against each other at the Granard Feis. He got the prize, but everybody knew that it was me played the best.

BRIAN : There's few of them alive now that mind of the Granard Feis. He got the prize, and there's no talk of you at all.

CONN : No talk of me at all?

BRIAN : It's said that since you settled down you lost your art.

CONN : And what had the men at Flynn's to say about that?

BRIAN : They bragged about you for a while, but the Sligomen put them down.

CONN : I wonder would we have time to go up, play a few tunes, and come back, while Maire would be doing something? I wonder if we would have time. It would be a pity not to give them fellows a lesson and close their ignorant mouths for them.

(ANNE *comes in with* MAIRE.) :

I thought you went somewhere and left Brian and myself here.

68

ANNE : We're going somewhere and Brian might come with us.

MAIRE (*at rack, making ready to leave*) : Everyone is going to Moynihan's.

CONN : It's a pleasant house, a pleasant house. Brian will make his ceilidh with me. We might go over a few tunes.

ANNE : Let Brian come where there are girls that might miss him.

MAIRE : Anne, you're a great one for keeping up the story that girls are always thinking about men.

ANNE (*crossing to BRIAN*) : And so they are. Just as men are always thinking about girls.

MAIRE : You'd make a good Ribbonman with your two-faced talk.

ANNE : Ribbonism and secret societies were denounced off the altar.

MAIRE : Goodness! The men will begin to think they've secrets worth telling.

ANNE : Have you secrets worth telling, Brian?

MAIRE : I daresay he has. There are foolish women in the world.

ANNE : Are you coming to Moynihan's, Brian?

BRIAN : I was thinking of going and now I am thinking of not going.

MAIRE : Come, Anne, till I deck you out.

(ANNE *moves centre to* MAIRE.)

Come here, daughter, don't wear flowers. I think they're unlucky. Here I am talking like this, and I going to a dance. I suppose I'll dance with seven or eight and forget what's on my mind. Everyone is going except the men here. Are you going out, Father?

CONN : I'm making a ceilidh with Brian.

MAIRE : Well, God be with you both. Come on, Anne.
          (MAIRE *takes down her shawl, and puts it over her head. She stands at the door, watching* ANNE, *who goes to* BRIAN.)
ANNE : Brian, what have you against Moynihans'?
BRIAN : Nothing at all. I may go in.
MAIRE : Come on, Anne. God be with you both.
          (MAIRE *and* ANNE *go out. They are heard talking for a while.* CONN *goes to the door.*)
CONN : Maire and Anne are turning the bohareen. Come on now. (*He takes the fiddle and wraps it up eagerly.*)
BRIAN : Ay, let's go.
CONN (*at door*) : I never forget. The Granard Feis is as fresh in my mind as the day I played at it. Shawn Heffernan, indeed! I never forget. I never forget.
          (CONN *and* BRIAN *go out.*)

CURTAIN

ACT TWO

The next day. The scene is as in previous
Act. It is now the forenoon.

(MAIRE *is seated at the fire in a listless attitude.* ANNE
is busy sweeping.)

MAIRE : We shouldn't have stayed at Moynihans' so late.

ANNE : Indeed it would have been better to go home, but I
was sure that Brian McConnell would come in.

MAIRE : Well, it was his loss if he didn't come. Maybe
there was one that I liked better.

ANNE (*turning to* MAIRE) : You couldn't like Connor Gilpatrick better than Brian McConnell.

MAIRE : Connor's the best-looking boy in the country.
Was it noticed that we were together often?

ANNE (*significantly*) : Peggy Carroll noticed it.

MAIRE : Well, the boy was glad to talk to me. Connor's a
good dancer and he has fine talk besides. If Brian
McConnell had come to the door, I wouldn't have
turned my head towards him. (*She rises and goes to
mirror.*)

ANNE : Sure you wouldn't compare a young boy like
Connor Gilpatrick with Brian McConnell?

MAIRE : I wouldn't have turned my head towards Brian.
O! never expect kindness from men. Why did you
let me stay on? (*turning to* ANNE) I'm afraid to look
at myself in the glass to-day.

(ANNE *disposes of broom. A pause.*)

You were hard on me, Anne, yesterday.

ANNE : I didn't like the way you talked to father.

MAIRE : I think I'm getting different to what I used to be. Well, I've reason to be sorry for what I did yesterday. (*She is at the window.*) Was Peggy Carroll vexed at the way I went on?

ANNE : She never took her eyes off the pair of you. You know she's very fond of Connor.

MAIRE (*going to* ANNE) : Anne, never remind me of my foolishness. (*She puts her arms round* ANNE.) I'm heartsick of myself to-day.

ANNE : I'll comb out your hair for you, and you'll look well enough. (*She takes comb from shelf.*)

MAIRE : Then you're expecting Brian McConnell?

ANNE : It's likely he'll come in to see if there's anything to be done.

MAIRE : I suppose he'll come in. (*Turning towards window.*) Gracious, how did father get out? He's coming up the path.

ANNE : Father's not up, surely? Maire, be easy with Brian McConnell when he comes in.

MAIRE : Father's coming up the path, Anne. (*Pause.*) Anne!

ANNE (*crossing to door*) : What is it, Maire?

MAIRE : Father wasn't in at all, last night.

ANNE : Then he went to Flynn's after all. (*Turning to* MAIRE.)

MAIRE : Ay, he went to Flynn's. (*She goes to fireplace.*)

ANNE : O, Maire, what will become of us all? (*Crossing to dresser.*)

MAIRE : I don't know. (*She sits on stool at fireplace.*)

ANNE : What will we do with him at all?

(CONN HOURICAN *appears at outside door.*)

CONN : God save you! (*He looks around and enters.*) Well, I came back to ye.

ANNE : You did, God help us! And we depending on you.

CONN : Did you hear what happened to me, before you attack me?

72

ANNE : What happened to you? What always happens to you? It's the bad way you always treated us.

CONN : I wonder that a man comes in at all! The complaints against him are like the Queen's Speech, prepared beforehand.

ANNE : Ever since I can remember, you treated us like that. Bringing us into drinking places and we little. It's well we got to know anything, or got into the way of being mannerly at all.

CONN : You know too much. I always said that. (*He leaves his fiddle on the table and moves towards fire.*) Is James Moynihan coming here to-day?

ANNE : No, he isn't coming here to-day.

CONN : Well, we can do without him. There's something to be done to-day. I said I'd do a bit of mowing, and I was thinking of that all along. (*He looks at* MAIRE). Did you hear what happened to me, Maire?

MAIRE : It's no matter at all.

CONN : I went over to Flynns', I may tell you.

ANNE : In troth we might have known that.

CONN (*crossing to* ANNE) : But did you hear what happened to me?

ANNE : How could we hear ; it was Maire went to the window, and there you were coming up the path ; and we thinking you were in bed, resting yourself.

CONN : I went to Flynns', but I had good reason for going there. Didn't you hear there was Sligomen in the town, Maire? Well, one of them was in the way of rewarding the prizes. I told you about the Feis; well, it's no matter now, I'll say no more about that. At all events, the man I mentioned wanted to know what music was in the country, so he sent a message to myself.

ANNE (*as satirical as she can be*) : That was kind of him.

73

CONN : It was. I could do no less than go. I'll rest myself
now and then get ready for the mowing. (*He goes
towards his room; turns again and watches* MAIRE.) Maire,
I'm sorry that you weren't on the spot. You might
have advised me. I couldn't think of where you went
or I'd have followed you. I had to make haste.

MAIRE : It's no matter at all now.

CONN (*moving to stairs*) : I'll stretch myself on the bed before
I begin work. Anne, did you say you were leaving
something in the room for me?

ANNE : I suppose I'll have to leave the tea in the room for
you. (*She gets a cup and saucer from the dresser, crosses
to hearth and pours out tea.*)

    (MAIRE *remains motionless.*)

CONN : Well, I have the pattern of daughters, anyway. I
wouldn't give this house for the praise of Ireland. No,
not if they carried me on their backs.

    (ANNE *takes tea up to the room.*)

It's a pity you weren't there, Maire. (*Crossing to
centre.*) Though of course I wouldn't bring you to
such a place. But they were decent fellows, decent,
warm-hearted fellows. If you were to see their faces
when I played "An Cailín Donn." I'll warrant they'll
be whistling it, though they never heard the tune
before. And the manners they have! I offered the
fiddle to one of them. " No," says he, " not a string
will I touch while the master of us is here." That's
something like the spirit.

    (ANNE *returns.* MAIRE *turns to* CONN *and is attentive.*)

But there, I won't fill myself up with false music
telling you about it all. (*He turns to go to room.*)

MAIRE : Bring up your fiddle.

CONN (*taking fiddle and going towards room again*) : It will be as
good as sound sleeping for me. I'll never forget it. Flynn
will never forget it. It will be the making of Flynn.

74

MAIRE (*rising*) : You've only your fiddle; we shouldn't forget that.

(CONN *goes up to the room.*)

ANNE : O, Maire, what will become of us at all? (*Looking after* CONN.)

MAIRE : He is very pleased with himself.
He has only his fiddle, we shouldn't forget that.

ANNE : It will be a long time till he does the like again.

MAIRE : It will be a long time, I suppose. Both of us might be in a different house and have different cares.

ANNE : That would be terrible. I'll never leave him, Maire.

MAIRE : You can't say the like now.

ANNE : Why?

MAIRE : How could you take such things upon you and life stretching out before you? You're not young enough, Anne. Besides, it's not what we say; it's what we feel. No, it's not what we feel either; it's what grows up in us.

ANNE : He might never do the like again. (*Placing hands affectionately on* MAIRE.)

MAIRE : Many's the time mother said that, and she and me lying together.

ANNE : Will we ever get out of it, Maire?

(JAMES *enters.*)

MAIRE : You have only a while to stay with us.

JAMES : God save you, girls!

ANNE (*crossing to James*) : O James, what will your father say if he hears of you giving us another day?

JAMES : My father took a stick in his hand this morning, and went off with himself.

MAIRE : You're welcome, James. (*Crossing towards him*). It was a pleasant time we had in your house last evening.

75

JAMES : I hope you liked the company, Maire. I'm afraid
there was very little to be called refined or scholarly,
and the conversation at times was homely enough.
But we did our best, and we were proud to see you.

MAIRE : Sit down, James.

(MAIRE *sits on stool.* JAMES *sits on settle.* ANNE *leans
against settle.*)

JAMES (*as he crosses to settle*) : Your father is outside, maybe?

MAIRE : No, he's above in the room.

JAMES : Yes, practising, I suppose. Them that have the gift
have to mind the gift. In this country there isn't much
thought for poetry, or music, or scholarship. Still, a
few of us know that a while must be spared from the
world if we are to lay up riches in the mind.

ANNE : I hope there's nothing wrong at home?

JAMES (*turning to* ANNE) : To tell you the truth, and to keep
nothing back, there is.

MAIRE : And what is it, James?

JAMES (*turning to* MAIRE) : Anne was talking to my father
last night.

ANNE : Indeed I was, and I thought him very friendly to
me.

JAMES : Ay, he liked you well enough, I can tell you that,
Anne. This morning when he took a stick in his hand,
I knew he was making ready for a journey, for the
horse is laid up. " Walk down a bit with me," he said,
" and we'll go over a few things that are in my mind."
Well, I walked down with him, and indeed we had a
serious conversation.

ANNE : Well?

JAMES : "Anne Hourican is too young," said my father;
" she's a neat girl, and a good girl, but she's too
young."

MAIRE : Sure in a while Anne will be twenty.

JAMES (*turning to* MAIRE) : Ten years from this father would still think Anne too young. And late marriages, as everybody knows, is the real weakness of the country.

ANNE : I thought your father liked me.

JAMES : He likes you well enough, but, as he says, " what would she be doing here and your sisters years older than herself?" There's truth in that, mind you. I always give in to the truth.

MAIRE : James Moynihan?

JAMES : Well, Maire?

MAIRE : Is Anne Hourican a girl to be waiting twenty years for a man like Sally Cassidy?

JAMES : God forbid, Maire Hourican, that I'd ask your sister to wait that length.

MAIRE : She hasn't got a fortune. We were brought up different to farmers, and maybe we never gave thought to the like.

JAMES : She has what's better than a fortune. (*He takes* ANNE'S *hand lovingly.*)

MAIRE : Why aren't your sisters married off?

JAMES : Big fortunes are expected with them.

MAIRE : And they look to your wife to bring a big fortune into the house?

JAMES : Ay, they do that.

MAIRE : You, James, ought to have some control in the house. You're the only son. Your father is well off. Get him to fortune off your sisters, and then bring Anne to the house.

JAMES : But how could I get father to fortune off the girls?

MAIRE : How? By waking up. You have the right. When we have the right, we ought to be able to do anything we like with the people around us.

JAMES : I give in to the truth of that, Maire.

MAIRE : What will come of you giving in to the truth of it? But sure you ought to remember Anne.

ANNE : James has the good way with people.

MAIRE (*crossing to door*) : Well, I suppose it will come out right for you in the end. You are both very deserving. But some time or another we have to take things into our own hands.

JAMES : Indeed that's true, Maire.

(CONN *appears on the stairs with fiddle and comes down.*)

CONN : I heard your voice, James, and I thought I'd come down. (*He moves to table.*)

ANNE (*holding* JAMES' *hand*) : Did you make any more songs, James?

JAMES : I have a song in my head since last night.

CONN (*putting fiddle on table*) : It's very good of you to come here again. I'll be out with you to-day.

JAMES : It'll be a good day from this on.

ANNE : The poem in the paper is lovely. I know it by heart.

JAMES : The next one I make will be ten times better. (*To* CONN.) Were you practising above, Mister Hourican?

CONN : Well, no, James, I wasn't practising. I was at a big gathering last night, and my hands are unstrung like.

ANNE : James!

(CONN *brings a chair from the table and places it opposite the fire.*)

CONN : We'll talk for a while, and then, I'll go out with you.

ANNE (*taking* JAMES' *arm*) : Come out with me for a minute.

(ANNE *and* JAMES *rise.*)

JAMES : I'll see you again, Mister Hourican.

(JAMES *and* ANNE *go out.*)

CONN : Well, God help us. (*He turns to go back to the room.*)

(MAIRE *comes down from back.*)

Are you going out, Maire?

MAIRE : No, I'm staying here. (*Sits on settle.*)

CONN (*aggrieved*) : Do you mind them two, how they went out together. (*Pause.*) I think I'll go out and see what's to be done about the place. (*He goes towards entrance and pauses at door.*) I broke my word to you, Maire.

MAIRE : I don't know what to say to you now.

CONN : It was the music and the strange faces that drew me.

MAIRE : I know that now.

CONN : It will be a long time till I break my word to you again.

MAIRE : I'll never ask for your word again.

CONN (*warmly*) : I can tell you this, Maire. (*Crossing to her*). There's many's the place in Ireland where Conn Hourican's word would be respected.

MAIRE : I'll never ask for your word again. You have only your fiddle, and you must go among people that will praise you. When I heard you talking of your listeners, I knew that. I was frightened before that. When I saw you coming, I went and sat there, and I thought the walls of the house were crowding in on me.

CONN : You were partly to blame, Maire. You left me there very lonesome.

MAIRE : I was to blame, I suppose. I should have treated you differently. Well, I know better now. Let you sit down and we'll talk together.

(CONN *sits on chair to left of settle.*)

What's to become of myself, I don't know. Anne and James Moynihan will marry, I hope. Neither of us have fortunes, and for that reason our house should be well spoken of.

CONN : Sure I know that. I wouldn't bring the shadow of a disgrace near us.

79

MAIRE : If the father isn't well spoken of, how could the house be well spoken of? They're big drinkers that go to Flynn's, and it's easy for the fiddler to get into the way of drinking.

CONN : I won't go to Flynn's when you put it that way.

MAIRE : I'll ask for no word. I'll let you know the real way of the house, and then trust you.

CONN : You're a good girl, Maire. I should have been said by you.

MAIRE : From this out, there will be dances at the school-house and the like of that. You could be playing at them.

CONN : None of the oul' people go to the like, and the young don't understand me nor my ways. God knows will I ever play again. That thought is often with me of late, and it makes me very lonesome.

MAIRE : That's foolishness.

CONN : I was very lonesome when you left me. You don't know how I was tempted, Maire. There was Brian McConnell putting on his coat to go to Flynn's, and talking of the Sligomen.

MAIRE (*startled*) : And was it to Flynn's that Brian McConnell went?

CONN : It was Brian that brought me to Flynn's.

MAIRE : Was it Brian McConnell that brought you to Flynn's?

CONN : It was.

MAIRE (*passionately*) : You must never go to Flynn's. (*She rises and moves to centre.*)

CONN : I'm ashamed of myself. Didn't I say that, Maire?

MAIRE (*with hardness*) : You must never go again.

CONN : And is a man to have no life to himself?

MAIRE : That's talk just. It's time you thought of your own place and your own children. It's time you gave up caring for the praise of foolish people.

80

CONN : Foolish people, did you say?

MAIRE : Ay, foolish people. You had all your life to yourself, and you went here and there, straying from place to
place, and caring only for the praise of foolish people.

CONN : God help you, if that's what you're thinking! Sure
the world knows that a man is born with the gift, and
isn't the gift then the sign of the grace of God? Foolish
people, indeed! Them that know the gift have some
of the grace of God, no matter how poor they may be.

MAIRE : You're always thinking of *them*. You never think
of your own. Many's the time your own cried tears
over your playing.

CONN (*passionately, starting up*) : I'll go out of the house.

MAIRE : Let you stay here.

CONN (*going towards entrance*) : I'll go out of the house, I tell
you.

MAIRE (*barring the way*) : No.
(CONN *goes over to the fire.*)

CONN : God help me that ever came into this country at all.
(*He sits down, with his hands resting on his stick.*) I had
friends once, and was well thought of; I can tell you
that, my daughter.

MAIRE : I know that.

CONN : Well, you can have your own way with me, now.
(*Pause.*)

MAIRE : Why won't you stay here? (*going to him and kneeling beside him.*) There's lots to be done here. Our fields
are a laughing-stock to the neighbours, they're that
poor and wasted. Let us put all our minds into working, and have a good place of our own.

CONN : Ay, and the grabbers and informers of this place
would think well of you then.

MAIRE : Who do you call grabbers and informers?

CONN : The people of this place. The people you want to
shine before.

81

MAIRE : I don't want to shine before the people. (*She rises.*)

CONN : I'm not saying against you, Maire.

MAIRE : You're wrong in thinking I want to shine at all.

CONN : Sure you go to every dance and ceilidh; and to every house where you can show off your face, and dancing and conversation.

MAIRE : Do I? Maybe I do. Every girl does the like.

CONN : I'm not saying against it.

(*Pause.*)

MAIRE : You think I'm like yourself, wanting the praise of the people.

CONN : And what's the harm if you do?

MAIRE : No harm at all. But I don't go to houses to show myself off.

CONN : Troth and you do, Maire.

MAIRE : I won't believe it. (*She turns to window—back to audience.*) (ANNE *comes in.*)

CONN : Had you a good night at Moynihan's, Anne?

ANNE : A sort of good night.

CONN : I was going to tell you about the man I met last night. He had a song about your grandmother.

ANNE : Was grandmother a great beauty, Father?

CONN : Honor Gilroy had good looks, and indeed she made the most of them.

MAIRE (*turning slightly*) : It's likely there was some to tell her she was showing off.

CONN : No one was to her liking unless they praised her.

(*A fiddle is heard in the distance outside playing " The Royal Blackbird."*)

ANNE : Ah, well, a fiddler ought to forgive that to a woman.

MAIRE : Fiddlers and women are all alike, but don't say that to him. And fiddlers and women oughtn't to be hard on each other.

82

CONN : Do you say that, Maire?
     (*The fiddle is heard nearer.*)

MAIRE : I say it, Father. (*She moves R.*)

CONN : God forgive me if I vexed you, Maire.

ANNE (*rising*) : It's clearing up now, Father, and you ought
    to go out to James.

CONN : I'll be glad enough to have the scythe in my hand
    after all.
     (*Fiddle very close. Enter* JAMES.)

JAMES : Some of the boys want to meet you. They have a
    fiddle with them.

CONN : I'll go out to them. (*He takes the fiddle and goes out.*)
    (JAMES *follows him out.*)

ANNE : What did you say to him?

MAIRE : He doesn't feel it at all. Father will always be the
    fiddler, no matter what we say. (*She crosses to fire.*)
     (*The fiddle outside stops.*)

ANNE : Maire. (*She sits on a chair.*) I was talking to James.
    He'll never be happy until we're under the one roof.

MAIRE : Anne, I'll be very lonesome for you.

ANNE : But sure I won't be far off, Maire.

MAIRE : Ay, but it's terrible to face things alone.
     (*The fiddle starts again and the playing is better.*)

ANNE : What's come over you to say that?

MAIRE : Oh, I oughtn't to say it. I'm always thinking about
    myself and father. (*She moves towards* ANNE *and sits.*)
    It's time I thought of you, Anne. You and James
    Moynihan——you suit each other. Things musn't be
    let come between you. His father will be going all
    over the country to make a match for him and
    quarrelling with James on the head of it.

ANNE : James will never give in to his father when it comes
    to me.

MAIRE : But delays and delays! We don't know what could
    happen when there are long delays.

ANNE : I'm frightened when you say things the like of that, Maire.

> *(The fiddle stops. Another fiddle takes up the same tune and slowly fades away.)*

MAIRE : Well, don't be. There are ways of persuading James' father.

ANNE : Maybe you know a way, Maire?

MAIRE : Maybe I do, then. *(She turns away.)*

> *(JAMES appears at the door holding it open for the entrance of CONN and JUSTIN REILLY.)*

CONN : Indeed it will be a great surprise to them to see you again, Justin Reilly! Here's Maire herself, and Anne that you disremember. Maire, here he is back to us! The young man that I used to give lessons to! How long would it be since then, Justin Reilly?

JUSTIN : Just four years, Master Hourican.

CONN : Just think of that, Maire, and now he's near-hand being priested.

> *(MAIRE greets him. JUSTIN REILLY is a young man whose dress already seems somewhat clerical. There is a holiday good humour about him; he looks assured and happy; one can believe he has found his vocation.)*

MAIRE : It's good of you to come to see us. Indeed you look as if you were within a while of being a priest.

CONN : He was far away too, Maire. In a college abroad.

JUSTIN : I'm all the way from Spain, from Salamanca, if you ever heard of the place.

CONN : Think of that, Maire! That's further than you or me will ever see.

ANNE : Even the wild geese come back to this little place.

JUSTIN : Even the wild geese, Anne.

CONN : I'll be leaving you here with Maire for a while, Justin. I promised the boys another tune. Come out with us, Anne; we'll be leaving you here together for a while.

84

MAIRE : Won't you sit down.

(CONN, ANNE *and* JAMES *go out.*)

JUSTIN : It's like old times hearing the fiddle on an Irish road.

MAIRE : What would you think of a girl like myself going the roads, Justin Reilly?

JUSTIN : Well, where would you be going to, Maire?

MAIRE : To Ardagh with my father, maybe.

JUSTIN : Oh, to be sure! The Feis will be there. But it won't be long till you're both home from it.

MAIRE : We ought to let him go. Amn't I right to think that, Justin?

JUSTIN : It would give the fiddler a new lease of life, I'm certain.

MAIRE : I thought we were settled here. I didn't want him to be on the roads again. I wanted him to be different from what he could be. It would give him a new lease of life, you said. Well, that's settled. This day week we'll be on the road.

JUSTIN : But why have you to go with your father to Ardagh?

MAIRE : It's because . . . Oh, I suppose it's because we were always together.

JUSTIN : Ay, you're the fiddler's child and the road has a hold on you.

MAIRE : Oh, no. No, indeed. I'd be desolate on the roads after this house. But do you know what I'm thinking of doing, Justin?

JUSTIN : Tell me, Maire.

(MAIRE *takes fireplace stool and moves nearer to* JUSTIN.)

MAIRE : Giving my sister this house and land. It wouldn't be that I'd be giving it up altogether. But Anne would have it and then she could get married to James Moynihan and not be waiting years and years, and not have anything come between them as might happen if

85

his father pressed on him. I'm just thinking about it. And what would you think of me doing the like?

JUSTIN : I couldn't tell you to deprive yourself of this shelter.

MAIRE : It wouldn't be just like that. It wouldn't be that I'd be without a shelter. Or my father, either. I want you to know that. And I want you to know another thing——

JUSTIN : What is it, Maire?

MAIRE : Do you know that I'm talking to you as if you were a priest already?

JUSTIN : Well, I have the vocation—I know that.

MAIRE : Yes, you have that. I won't say "Bless me, Father," or anything like that to you.

JUSTIN : No. You mustn't get in advance of my faculties, you know. (*Both laugh.*)

MAIRE : I'm discontented with myself—since to-day—last night—yesterday.

JUSTIN : In a day we can change. I know that. But maybe I ought to ask you something.

MAIRE : Yes, ask.

JUSTIN : You tell me your sister will get married. And yourself? There's surely one who wants you?

MAIRE : There is. But I don't know what he would do. I don't know what I would do.

JUSTIN : I suppose that's the case with many a girl.

MAIRE : But I'm different, I think. Aren't there men that one can trust, that one can depend on? If there is a man that's strong, can't he have a heart for what I think about?

JUSTIN : Then I'll have to ask you another thing, child— have you love for him?

MAIRE : No matter what I'm doing, no matter what I'm talking about, it's he that's in my mind at all hours.

86

JUSTIN : You would leave this house and land to your sister,
   you would go with your father to Ardagh . . .
MAIRE : I would. It's settled now.
JUSTIN : And then if the fiddler wanted to go on, fiddlers
   do?
MAIRE : Ah, but you wouldn't be able to tell me now what
   I ought to do.
JUSTIN : Yes, I would.
MAIRE : I'll remember what you tell me.

   (*The fiddle is heard in the distance playing " The
   Royal Blackbird."*)

JUSTIN : Look into yourself. You are one of the people who
   would know what they would be happiest doing.
   Happiest. Maybe I don't mean that. But most like
   yourself doing. The roads are harsh; the places you'd
   rest in are ill-fitted for you. But there are no dangers
   for the like of you on the roads of Ireland . . .
MAIRE : I know the roads—I know them well.
JUSTIN : I'm proud that you let me know what's in your
   mind.

   (*The music is now very close.* CONN *enters with*
   JAMES.)

CONN : You're a scholar, Justin Reilly, and maybe you can
   tell me why the music they're playing is such a proud
   and lifting tune?
JUSTIN : God knows I cannot, Master Hourican. It ought
   not to be, for the " Royal Blackbird " was made about
   the king who never won anything.
CONN : Do you tell me that. Well, it was always before
   him to win something, wasn't it; and to win something grander and finer than any king ever won
   before?
JUSTIN (*indulgently*) : No doubt, Master Hourican.
CONN : It's the tune for me and I'll be playing it often.

(JUSTIN *stands near the window with* MAIRE *and* ANNE.)

JAMES (*to the girls*) : The men down the road were saying that your father took the victory from all last night.

(*The music outside stops.*)

CONN : Them poor Connacht fiddlers! Still, I'm sorry for them. They'll never be able to hold up their heads again.

JAMES : Sure I'd have it in a ballad that would be sung in their own towns. It would be well worth putting into a ballad.

CONN : Well, indeed, it would make a right good ballad, James.

JAMES : I'd like to make a ballad about it that would be sung all over Connacht.

CONN : And why wouldn't you do it, James? Sure it would be the making of you. It would be sung all over Ireland and your name to it. (*He goes on talking to* JAMES, *each of them getting more excited.*)

JUSTIN : But wouldn't it be a strange thing to break off a marriage just because her brother didn't like him?

(ANNE *nods sympathetically.* MAIRE *turns away.*)

MAIRE : Here we are talking about Brian McConnell again!

JUSTIN : But wouldn't it be a strange thing? My friend, Canavan and Rose . . .

MAIRE : The McConnells are wild people.

CONN : Did you hear that, Maire? Did you hear that, Anne?

JAMES : I'm saying I'd like to make a ballad about Conn Hourican's victory.

ANNE : Will it be a poem or a ballad, James?

(*He seats himself near dresser, gets a piece of paper before him while* ANNE *leans over him.*)

CONN : If you had it this night week, we could bring the boys to the place. What do you say to that, Maire? We could bring the boys here this night week to hear James Moynihan's ballad.

(JUSTIN *stands looking out of the window. Again the music is heard outside.*)

MAIRE : This night week will be the Feis at Ardagh.

(ANNE *rises and stands at fire.*)

CONN : The Feis at Ardagh?

MAIRE : Maybe you'll be going to it this night week. (*She crosses to* CONN.)

CONN : Sure you're not joking with me, Maire?

MAIRE : I'm not joking. (*She goes up to* CONN'S *room.*)

CONN : God forgive me if I vexed you, Maire. (*Moving towards* ANNE.) Anne, jewel!

ANNE : Yes.

CONN : Had Maire anything to say about Ardagh?

ANNE : We weren't talking about that at all.

(MAIRE *comes to the doorway of* CONN'S *room with another fiddle.* JUSTIN *singing to the air of " The Royal Blackbird," which is being played off.*)

JUSTIN (*singing*) : But his cause I'll advance
                    In Spain and in France.
                    Good luck to my Blackbird wherever
                         he'll be!

Still, Master Hourican a King without subjects—if there's any poorer case, I don't know of it.

(*The music off ceases*).

CONN : There might be, there might be, Justin. Take my own case . . . Now put yourself in my place. You went to college; you read books in Latin, and you're near hand being priested. Well, now supposing . . . supposing this, Justin Reilly . . . I'm telling you what might be your own case. Supposing you came back to this place as a scholar and a priest and all that you think you're going to be, and then you never went

89

near a bishop, and never had a chapel of your own, and never said Mass or stood upon an altar. Do you understand what I'm saying, Justin? And you a priest by all rights?

(JUSTIN *makes a sign of assent.* MAIRE *listens attentively.*)

Supposing, Justin, something came and reminded you of all your were to be? You, maybe, at the time sitting in your house and reading the paper out, and telling the people of all that was happening in the world. Just doing that and nothing else, for all your scholarship and all you were through. I'm thinking that you'd rise up and you'd say ' No matter what comes or goes, I'll go out of this; I'll find a bishop if he was on the very edge of Ireland, and I'll say to him, I have the right to say Mass; sure there must be some congregation for me ! '

JUSTIN : So that's what you want to do, Master Hourican? Look for your congregation.

CONN : The man of art must have his listeners, too.

(MAIRE *goes to cupboard below window to get another fiddle.*)

JUSTIN : I have enough of the fiddler to know it's a good comparison you're making.

(MAIRE *comes down to* CONN *and puts the fiddle into his hands.*)

MAIRE : Here's the fiddle that is your favourite.

CONN : The Granard fiddle.

MAIRE : The fiddle you'll be taking to Ardagh this day week.

ANNE : And will he be going to Ardagh this day week?

MAIRE : He will, and I'll be going with him.

CONN : How well she bethought of the Granard fiddle.

JUSTIN : But you'll be better off than a priest, Conn; your
    daughter will be with you. She's a fine, wild girl, too,
    Maire Hourican.
MAIRE : Wild, did you say, Justin?
JUSTIN : Wild like some of the tunes your Father plays.
CONN : Isn't that what I'm always saying? Anne is like the
    tame pigeon about the house, and Maire is like the
    pigeon of the woods.
MAIRE : God help me if I am to be judged by my Father
    and my confessor!

CURTAIN

ACT THREE

A week later. The scene is as in previous acts.
The table is laid for a meal. The time is near
sunset.

> (CONN *is seated at the left of the table.* JAMES *is at the
> back and* MAIRE *is at the right.* ANNE *is at the right of
> back.*)

CONN : However it is, I could never play my best in this
place. The houses are too scattered, I often think. And
it doesn't do for the fiddler to remain too long in the
one place. The people get too used to him. Virgil
made better songs than any man, but if Virgil was
sung in the fairs constant, divil much heed would be
given his songs.

JAMES : Now, I often thought of that. How do you think
you'll do at Ardagh?

CONN : I think I'll do very well at Ardagh, James.

JAMES : Everything ready for the start?

CONN : Ay, and it's near time for going. I'm playing very
well, lately, James. It's the thought of being before
people who'll know music. If I was staying in this
place any longer, James, I'd put my fiddle in the
thatch, and leave it there for the birds to pick holes in

JAMES : But won't you be back here after the Feis at
Ardagh?

CONN : Oh, I will, for a while any way.

JAMES : And would you be going off again after a while?

CONN : I'm thinking that when my daughters are settled
I'll have the years before me. There's many's the place
in Ireland that I never saw, town and country side.

92

ANNE (*sitting at fireplace on floor*) : I suppose it's on account
of Maire going with father, but all last night I was
dreaming about the road! I thought about grassy
ditches by the roadside where Maire and myself used
to find the young birds. Imagine that! I dreamt I was
walking by the side of the road and under the elm
trees. The young jackdaws and crows were fallen out
of the nests in the branches above, and I was chasing
them the same as I chased them when I was little on the
roads. And I heard Maire's voice calling me not to
chase the young birds that were hopping thru' the
grass. (*She breaks the poetic mood.*) What's come over
me, Maire?

MAIRE : It won't be like the way it was when we were little.
There be changes here and there and everywhere.

CONN : Tell me, James Moynihan, is your father satisfied
with the settlement that Maire's making for yourself
and Anne?

JAMES : My father is very well satisfied.

(ANNE *gives a cup of tea to* JAMES.)

CONN : And so he ought to be, James Moynihan . . . wel
satisfied, now that Maire is making over the house and
land to the one you'll marry.

JAMES : What would you think of a row of trees planted
before the door?

CONN : They might be very becoming, James.

JAMES : My father was saying that the front of the house
looked very bare.

CONN : A row of trees, when they'd grow up, would make
a great difference.

JAMES : That's what my father was saying. And I'll tell
you what else I thought of doing. I'll make a path
down to the road, and with the row of trees planted,
the place will be well worth looking at.

93

MAIRE : We won't know the place when we come back to it. (*She rises.*) I never look at the place as my own, somehow. Speak to James, Father, and tell him he has all your will of the place. (*She goes to bedroom.*)

CONN : Indeed you have, James, and we're glad and over-glad that Anne will be settled here with a steady boy the like of yourself. And when Maire comes back—when Maire comes back (*he rises and goes to doorway*) —she'll find everything well and prosperous, I'll engage.

JAMES : And now that it's in Anne's name my father will be glad to stock the place. He thinks very little of the stock you have.

CONN (*looking out of the door*) : I never saw them horses before . . . the horses in the field outside our own. Three fine horses.

(JAMES *goes over to doorway to look out behind* CONN.)

JAMES : They're Brian McConnell's horses. Aye, in troth, the three of them are his! And they were saying he sold them to officers from the Emperor of Russia.

CONN : They're fine horses. I'll say that much for them. It's good for sore eyes to look at them. (*He goes out and stands outside window.*)

JAMES : Ah, well, the blossoms won't be off the sloe-bush yonder before Conn Hourican and Maire will be back to us. (*He crosses to fire.*) As for myself I'm often taken with the thought of the road. Going to the fair on a bright morning, I often thought I'd leave everything one side and follow the road. The rambler's in me, I think.

ANNE : Oh, James!

JAMES : But, of course, I wouldn't give in to the thought at all. No indeed, Anne, I wouldn't. May you never come to think, Anne, that you made a bad match when you took James Moynihan.

94

ANNE : I was never fond of anyone but yourself. (*She commences to clear the table.*)

JAMES : I never cared for anyone after I saw you.

ANNE : I used to hear . . .

JAMES : That I was fond of the girl who kept the newspaper shop in the town?

ANNE : Used you talk to her?

JAMES : The elbows were worn out of my coat with leaning on the counter to talk to her . . . and to read the papers that were spread out. But she married a policeman. He was a friend of mine, too. It was me got him the words and music for " I'll hang my harp on a Willow Tree " . . . a song he was always looking for.

ANNE : Did you make any songs about that girl?

JAMES : No, Anne, I did not.

ANNE : I'm glad of that. I'm glad you made songs about nobody but myself. (*Folding tablecloth.*)

JAMES (*crossing to her*) : And are you content to marry me in Ardagh while Maire and your father are there?

ANNE : It, James——it's a great trial for a girl to face marriage, but I'm fond of you.

(*They kiss. Afterwards* JAMES *goes upstage.* ANNE *puts cloth in dresser drawer.*)

JAMES : My sister, Grace, will be here with you until you go to Ardagh. (*He looks out.*) I can't help but think what a nice rise of ground this house is on. Did you ever have anything else in the garden but gooseberry bushes?

ANNE : They're here ever since my grandmother's time.

JAMES : There's lots that would grow there in place of gooseberry bushes. My father said there couldn't be any better beds for cabbages.

(ANNE *goes to* JAMES *and takes his hand.*)

ANNE : And now you'll come out with me, James, for there's something I want to show you. There's a new calf and it's the littlest you ever saw.

JAMES : Ah, you'll see what my father means when he says your stock is not of the best. (*As they both go outside.*) He'll improve all that, you may be sure.

> (*After* ANNE *and* JAMES *have gone,* CONN *enters from outside.* MAIRE *comes down the stairs with a document. She goes to the dresser for the pen and ink and brings them to the table. She sits at table, centre.*)

CONN : And now we're letting another come into the place. Well, Honor Gilroy's house and land have been brought to many people. What paper is that, Maire?

MAIRE : It's a paper I've to put my name to. It's about giving the place to ANNE. James' father wants me to put my name on the paper. (*She commences to sign.*)

> (CONN *crosses to fire and sits.*)

CONN : Well, isn't James' father the Councillor with his paper and his signing! Well, well, I wouldn't put that past the Moynihans nor any of the rest of them in this place. Well, Anne will be settled.

MAIRE (*rising*) : Yes, the girl that I brought back from the roads will be settled here. (*She puts the document inside her bodice.*)

CONN : And yourself, Maire?

MAIRE (*going to half-door*) : I'm very fond of Aughnalee . . . the fields and the trees and the fairy thorns and all! I'm very fond of every turn of it.

CONN : And there's one will keep you here! And after that . . .

MAIRE (*turning towards him*) : You're thinking that after . . . when I'm the same as Anne will be . . . settled as they say . . . you'll go on the roads by yourself.

CONN : Brian McConnell's horses are to be seen from here.

MAIRE : But what do I know of Brian McConnell, after all!

CONN : Brian is wild, but he's freehanded.

MAIRE : Wild and freehanded? Men are like that! But that's not the sort of man I want to look to now!

CONN : There's a story about an ancient forefather of Brian McConnell that always comes into my mind when I see anything belonging to him.

MAIRE : What's the story? Maybe I never heard it.

CONN : They tell it for a saying that the McConnells have.

MAIRE : Tell it to me. (*She kneels beside him.*)

CONN : He was in a wood one day, this forefather of Brian, and he killed a deer. Then the white hound that had the deer in chase came and McConnell caught and held the hound. And then the lord who was hunting came and said to him, " Give *me* the deer and give the hound for having chased it." But McConnell said, " Let him who has the strongest hand take the white hound *and* the deer." Oh, I'm sure McConnell had the strong hand, the hand that would let nothing go. And so it's with them ever since. They take both the deer and the hound.

MAIRE : I saw Brian break horses! (*Pause*). It will be a change for us when we come back to the place.

CONN : And what do they know about music in Flynn's? Young Corney Miles was there, and you'd think from what the men said there was never the like of young Corney for playing, and the boy isn't three years at the fiddle.

MAIRE : Father, stay here where the shelter is.

CONN : Sure I'd be getting oul', and staying by the chimney corner with no one to talk to, for Anne after a while would have too much of her own care, and yourself . . .

MAIRE (*turning away*) : Who knows . . . Who knows about myself? Father, stay here. The people are kinder than you think.

CONN : But what has Conn Hourican the fiddler to do with them, anyway. Ah, why don't you know this, Maire? One is always meeting new life on the roads.

MAIRE (*rising*) : The like of you, the like of the fiddler, is always meeting new life on the roads.

CONN : The house took too much hold on you, Maire.

MAIRE (*moving away*) : The house wasn't for you, and it wasn't for me, I'm beginning to think. (*Pause*). If you took to the roads I'd think I ought to be with you, for we were always together.

CONN : No, for there's one would keep you here.

(*Offstage* JAMES *commences to whistle "the Blackbird."*)

MAIRE : Ah, what do I know about him? I saw him break horses and I knew him to go against what he knew was my wish! (*emotionally*). But why will we be talking like this, for I'll bring you back whatever comes or goes!

(*She goes to the door.* JAMES *comes to the window and, still whistling, pushes it open.*)

CONN : What is it, James?

JAMES : There are men where the horses are . . . they aren't men from this part of the country.

CONN (*impatiently*) : Well, well, what about them, James?

JAMES : They are asking if you'd play for them . . . on account of your leaving they want to hear you.

CONN : I wonder if they're County Leitrim men? I'll take my fiddle and go to them. (*He takes his fiddle from the shelf and talks to* JAMES *as he goes.*) I'm playing a great deal better this while back. Since I thought of starting for Ardagh I'm playing better. It's the thought of being with people who know music that makes me play to my own satisfaction. (*Exit*).

MAIRE (*at window*) : His horses are still in sight, Brian McConnell's horses! Maybe without my seeing him or hearing him, Brian McConnell will be away with them, away as far as where the Emperor of Russia lives!

(BRIAN MCCONNELL *comes to the door, a riding crop in his hand.*)

You're welcome, Brian, even if there's only myself here to welcome you. We were all watching your horses. You're taking them very far away, aren't you?

BRIAN : They're going far, but I wouldn't say I'm going that far.

MAIRE : Changes, changes! (*She sits*). There were never so many changes since I came here! I declare it's the same as if the prophecies of Columcille were coming true, with everything different so that nothing will be the same again! Why don't you come to the fire, Brian?

(*He comes centre.*)

Now this house is going to be Anne's——Anne's and James Moynihan's. They'll be married shortly——in Ardagh where my father and myself will be.

(*The fiddle is played outside.*)

BRIAN : Your father is going—— I know that much.

MAIRE : Changes, changes! Anne was dreaming about the roads. You'd never think she would, she's that settled in herself. And I was thinking of things on the road, too. You're not going as far as your horses are going, but you're going from this place, aren't you, Brian McConnell?

BRIAN (*harshly*) : Nobody knows what I'll be doing.

MAIRE : What were you doing since I saw you? Making quarrels, maybe?

BRIAN (*hotly*) : Why are you saying that? (*Coming towards her.*) Was any of them telling about me?

MAIRE : What else would you be doing with the strong hand and the wild heart?

99

BRIAN : That's as if you were talking about somebody you saw at a fair. You don't know me. Many's the time I left the spade in the ground and went across the bogs and the rushes to think of you.

MAIRE : It's easy taking a girl's heart with words!

BRIAN : I'd have jewels and gold for you, I'd have ships on the sea for you.

MAIRE (*moving centre*) : It's easy taking a girl's heart with the words of a song! What else have you to say to me? (*Turning away*). Oh, Brian, my father wants to go on the roads!

(MAIRE *goes to window*. BRIAN *follows*.)

BRIAN : That's the sort he is, Conn Hourican.

MAIRE : To go by himself from place to place!

BRIAN : It's the life of a fiddler to be on the roads.

MAIRE : But how much of my life was in thinking of him!

BRIAN : Let your father go.

MAIRE : Who else have I got?

BRIAN : Me that's before you, Maire. Don't you think of me at all?

MAIRE : Ah, since I knew you, I neither laughed or cried but on account of you.

BRIAN : Now that you say a thing like that, you'll find I'm easy to deal with, Maire.

MAIRE : My father . . .

BRIAN : Oh, let your father go where he wants to go, and come with me.

MAIRE : Ah, I want to hear you say more than that!

BRIAN : I'll let my horses go with the officers that came for them. I'll have the full of my hands of gold. You'll see what I'll do. I'll build a house for you, and it will be white and fine.

MAIRE : That's what you're thinking of, is it, Brian?

BRIAN : Day by day, from this day, I'll be raising a house for you.

100

MAIRE : Oh, that's something for me to hear. You'll be building a house and I thought you'd be going over the country getting into quarrels and destruction of every kind.

BRIAN (*hotly*) : Who told you? Who keeps talking to you about me?

MAIRE (*placatingly*) : No one, Brian. Indeed the people don't know you. " He who has the strong hand, let him take the white hound *and* the deer." They say things like that about you, and they don't know you at all. But what you'll be doing will be different from what they think.

BRIAN (*putting his arms about her*) : I'll be building a house— aye, to have you in it, Maire Hourican.

MAIRE : So then you'll be asking for my promise?

BRIAN : Give me your promise before you go to Ardagh.

MAIRE : If I gave you my promise now, I'd have great delight in coming back to this place.

BRIAN : Oh, God knows I want it now and I want it worse than any man ever wanted a girl's promise. There are my horses, and you don't know what's before them or me! Leave over thinking of anything else, and think that if heaven opened before me you'd come between me and heaven.

MAIRE : I'm fond of this place, Brian.

BRIAN : And you need leave it——you need never leave it. Who wants you more than I do?
        (*The fiddle ceases.*)

MAIRE : Isn't it strange that I'm leaving? (*She breaks away from him.*) There, I keep on talking as if I wasn't coming back! That's strange, too.

BRIAN (*coming to her*) : All would be settled, all would be easy for us, if you would give me your promise.

MAIRE : But I'm going. This very day I'm going to Ardagh with my father.

101

BRIAN : It would be easy for me to be with you and Conn, going that far with you.

MAIRE : Oh, That's it! We'll talk about it on the road, you going beside us, leaving your horses in the field beyond ours. But you won't leave them there! You'll let the officers take them for the full of your hands in gold. Isn't that so, Brian? (*She is now standing at the door.*)

BRIAN : Give me your promise—now—this minute.

MAIRE : There's the blackbird! I'll hear him every evening along the road, and I'll think I'm a day nearer to the time when I'll be back.

BRIAN : Don't be putting me off with songs. It's not what I'm thinking of, and you must know that.

MAIRE : Do you know where I saw you first, Brian?

BRIAN : Where was it, my girl?

MAIRE : Where you were breaking horses. There was one horse that took you up and down the field. The poor beast was covered with foam and sweat . . . I must have thought that, for I was not near enough to see.

BRIAN : That stallion!

MAIRE : A stallion! Dangerous!

BRIAN : He was the best around here. You never saw him before that!

MAIRE : Well, I saw him then, didn't I?

BRIAN : You're not one of the girls who brought their father's mare to the stallion!

MAIRE : My father has no mare.

BRIAN : It was strange about that stallion. I never saw the like before. I was there when he came to a mare once. She kicked him.

MAIRE : Hurt him?

BRIAN : There was a way of hurting him. His spirit, maybe. It was that mare that broke him. And then I broke him for work or riding.

102

MAIRE : I thought he was covered with foam and sweat, and I couldn't see that.

BRIAN : But you remember that stallion and myself.

MAIRE (*as if held by the scene*) : I was afeard of you when I saw you that time. Sure I thought it was you and not the horse that would trample us all down! I wanted to be where you couldn't see me. I wasn't afeard of you in times after that! Maybe I thought I could bring you not to go at things the way of a horse-breaker, Brian. Ah, but I was afeard of you again! That was when you took the fiddler to Flynn's. I thought you were reaching across him and trying to tame me.

BRIAN : That would be a strange thing for me to do!

MAIRE : I was a strange one to think of it.

BRIAN : Sit down now and let me talk to you.

> (*But* MAIRE *remains standing.*) (*She sings.*)
> I know where I'm going,
> I know who's going with me,
> I know who I love,
> But the dear knows who I'll marry.

MAIRE : Are your brothers with you, Brian?

BRIAN : Out there, do you mean?

MAIRE : Oh, no. They're strangers out there, aren't they? Followers of yours? But when you'll be building the house, your brothers will be with you? (*Singing.*)
> I'll have stockings of silk
> Shoes of fine green leather,
> Combs to buckle my hair,
> And a ring for every finger.
> You haven't said anything for a minute.

BRIAN : Sit beside me and we'll talk of something else.

MAIRE :
> Feather beds are soft,
> Painted rooms are bonny,
> But I'd leave them all,
> To go with my love Johnny.
>
> (*The fiddle stops.*)

And won't your brothers be with you, Brian?

BRIAN : No.

MAIRE : Not in building the house?

BRIAN : But, nor in anything else.

MAIRE : You quarrelled with them?

BRIAN : They went against me—that's what they did.

MAIRE : No brothers with you—no one with you at all!

BRIAN : What do I care who'll be with me when you'll be with me?

MAIRE : It's slow and slow I'll be in coming back.

BRIAN : Listen, my proud girl. I'll ask you for the last time that you give me a promise. The only promise I'll ask of you is that you come back here.

MAIRE : Promise? (*Crossing to him.*) I'll give my promise to no man.

BRIAN : Think well before you say that! I'm asking little of you, I'm asking little, I that had only yourself to think of for days and months.

MAIRE : I to give my promise to you—no!

BRIAN : It's only . . . only that you come back here.

MAIRE : If it were even less than that, I'd give no promise to you.

BRIAN : Look out on the field there and see my three fine horses!

MAIRE : Not for the horses of yours will I give a promise! Not for the men with you will I give you a promise.

BRIAN : Maire Hourican!

MAIRE : You've come to say good-bye to me—that's what you've come for.

BRIAN : Why do you think I came with horses and men?

MAIRE : Here? You didn't come here with horses and men. You came as you always came and I gave you a welcome.

BRIAN : I came with horses and with men that are strangers here, that will give me all the help I'll ask of them.

MAIRE : You're not going to conquer us, are you?

BRIAN : Listen to me, Maire Hourican! You and me know of many a girl that was carried off by a man that wanted her more than she thought she wanted him.

MAIRE : You wouldn't take me off against my will—you wouldn't do that to me, Brian McConnell?

BRIAN : And who told you I wouldn't? Come with me— with your own will in it—come with me now, and the grandest wedding that ever was will be in the place that I will take you to.

MAIRE : And who told you I was the sort you could do this to?

BRIAN : Your head will be upon my pillow, one way or another.

MAIRE : You think you could sweep me out of this house and away from my father and sister and all my well-wishers! You think you can carry me across the mountain, and that then I would marry you because you carried me off! Yes, I know there were many that were married that way. You may call and the men with you may come up with their horses. But I'm not afraid of you at all. I thought I was frightened of you, but I'm not.

BRIAN : Yet I'll take you for all the spirit you show. I'll take you, but ever afterwards I'll be tender with you and let you have the rule over me.

MAIRE (*turning from him*) : Call them or whistle to them! The men the other side won't hear you. They're listening to my father's music.

(BRIAN *takes her up and carries her to the door. He holds her but does not carry her outside.*)

Carry me across that doorstep and I'll hate you so much that all my life I'll mock you. (*She breaks from him and comes down to the fire.*) Away with you now! Away with you to the men you brought with you to see me give in to you, and to see me ride behind you, holding your coat. Away with you! I put you from me like water that things were washed in. Away with you!

BRIAN : Stay here, you! I'm not as hard-set as I thought I was.

MAIRE—Because I'm not the one to hold your coat when you're making flight across the mountain.

BRIAN : However it is, stay here, you. Aye, but say something to me. Don't you care enough about me to tell me what to do with myself?

MAIRE : Go with your horses!

(BRIAN *throws the riding crop at his feet.*)

BRIAN : It's a far place; I'd be a long time getting there.

MAIRE : Well, that's what I tell you to do—go with your horses.

(*The fiddle ceases playing.* JAMES *and* ANNE *enter from outside.*)

JAMES (*coming down R.*) : Brian, you must come to your horses. The men want to be leaving.

BRIAN : If I go without a word from her, I'll never come back.

MAIRE : Go to your horses, Brian.

BRIAN : And go with them?

MAIRE : Maybe you'll have thought where you go that will make you know that your strong hand is the part that's least good to you.

BRIAN : Whatever I may come to think, I'll go now.

106

ANNE : You and Brian McConnell can't be parting? Oh, can you, Maire?

MAIRE : Say nothing to me about it now!

ANNE : I haven't the heart to say one thing or another about it.

BRIAN (*picking up the crop*) : I'll be going with my horses now.

ANNE : I'll expect you back if no one else will. I'll expect you back as far away as you're going. Even the wild geese come back to this little place and the lakes that are in it.

BRIAN : Tell your sister that Ireland is not as wide a place as she thinks it is. (*He goes.*)

(*The lights begin to dim inside as the sun sets.*)

ANNE (*coming down to* MAIRE *with a bunch of flowers*) : We gathered these for you, Maire, they be woodbine. We thought you'd be glad for them, the flower of the road.

(CONN *comes to the doorway and looks out on the horizon as he enters.*)

CONN : It's strange to be looking over the door and the sun setting for our journey.

MAIRE : Now, Father——

CONN : I know what you'll say, it's time to make ready.

MAIRE : Your coat is laid on the bed and the Granard fiddle is beside it.

CONN : Aye, indeed. I heard the Angelus when I was out. (*He goes up to his room.*)

(MAIRE *takes the paper from her bosom and hands it to* ANNE.)

MAIRE : Here it is, Anne, all signed to you and may you be lucky with it. (*She goes to her room.*)

(JAMES *crosses to* ANNE *and gloats over paper.*)

JAMES : My father will believe it now. Even the strip of bog beside his own is in it.

107

ANNE : And the dell that has the hazel nuts.

JAMES : The grass ought to be sweet there. Did you ever have sheep on it? But my father will have the black-faced ones over there as soon as he claps his eyes on this.

ANNE : You make me think about what your father minds. But that I've a good sister is what I ought to always think about.

(CONN *comes down from the room ready for the road.*)

CONN : God keep you, Anne, from this until I see you again.

(MAIRE *enters.*)

MAIRE (*to* ANNE) : Tell Brian McConnell that when we meet again maybe we can be kinder to each other.

CONN : My heart is unquiet for you, Maire.

MAIRE (*crossing to rack for her shawl*) : It need not be so.

CONN : And would you follow the road with me? It's not to one or two places I'll be going but to play wherever there's a crowd that knows music. To play in Ulster and in Munster, in Leinster and Connacht, in all parts and territories of Ireland.

MAIRE : If I lay my head down in a poor place, won't I rise up next day with my mind wide, with new things coming to me, with the day to think on what I got to know?

ANNE : Ireland is not as wide as you think—you won't forget that saying.

MAIRE : But the place Brian has gone to is wide. There will be two widths between us, and it takes a man that is faithful to come over the two widths. Don't be grieving that we're going from you. In a while your own care will begin.

(*She goes to door.*)

CONN : Well, here's Conn Hourican the fiddler going on
his travels again. I'm leaving the house behind me,
and maybe the time will come when I'll be climbing
hills and seeing this house with tears in my eyes. I'm
leaving the land behind me, too; but what's the land
after all against the music that comes from the far,
strange places, when the night is on the ground and the
bird in the grass is quiet? No man knows how his own
life will end, but them that have the gift have to
follow the gift.

(MAIRE *and* CONN *go out.* MAIRE *closes the door.*)

FINIS.

Thomas Muskerry

A play in four acts

Characters

THOMAS MUSKERRY, *the Master of Garrisowen Workhouse.*
MRS. CRILLY, *his daughter.*
CROFTON CRILLY, *his son-in-law.*
ALBERT CRILLY, *his grandson.*
ANNA CRILLY, *his granddaughter.*
JAMES SCOLLARD, *Thomas Muskerry's successor.*
FELIX TOURNOUR, *the porter at the Workhouse Lodge.*
MYLES GORMAN, *a blind piper.*
CHRISTY CLARKE, *a boy reared in the Workhouse.*
PETER MACNABO, *an old friend of Muskerry.*
SHANLEY, MICKIE CRIPES, *paupers in the Workhouse.*
AN OLD MAN
BARTHOLOMEW VINCENT MORANN, *a photographer.*

Scene : Garrisowen, a town in the Irish Midlands.

Time : The early nineteen hundreds.

112

ACT ONE   SCENE ONE

The Master's Office in Garrisowen Workhouse. It is partly an office, partly a living-room. To the right is a door opening on a corridor, and, in the back, left, a door leading to the Master's apartment. There is an iron stove down from back and towards right and a big grandfather's clock back towards door of apartment. A basket arm-chair down from stove, and a wooden chair beside it. There is a desk against wall left, and an office stool before it. Down from the desk a table on which is a closed desk. On table are books, papers and files. On wooden chair a heap of news-papers. There is a rack beside corridor door, and on the rack a shawl, an old coat, a hat, and a bunch of big keys. In the corner, right, is a little cabinet, and on it a small mirror. Above the door of the apartment is a picture of Daniel O'Connell. The grandfather's clock is ticking audibly. It is 8.45 p.m. The gas over the desk is lighted.

CHRISTY CLARKE, a youth of about seventeen, is seated in the arm-chair, reading. His clothes are threadbare, but brushed and clean. He looks studious. The clock ticks on, the boy reads, but with little attention. At the corridor door there is a knocking. Christy Clarke turns slightly. The door opens and a tall man in the ugly dress of a pauper is seen. The man is FELIX TOURNOUR. He carries in a bucket of coal. He performs this action like one who has acquired the habit of work under an overseer. In his pauper dress he presents an ugly figure. His scanty beard is coal black. He has a wide mouth and discoloured teeth. His forehead is narrow and bony. He is about forty-five.

TOURNOUR (*in a harsh voice, after looking around*): Is he not back yet?

CHRISTY (*without stirring*) : Is who not back yet?

TOURNOUR (*crossing to stove*) : The Master, I'm talking about. I don't know where he does be going these evenings. (*He shovels coals into the stove.*)

CHRISTY : And what is it to you where he does be going?

TOURNOUR : It's not your office to take me up like that. You're poorhouse rearing, even though you are a pet. Will he be sitting up here to-night, do you know?

CHRISTY : What's that to you whether he will or not?

TOURNOUR : If he's sitting up late, don't you think he'll want more coals on the fire?

CHRISTY : Well, the abstracts will have to be finished to-night.

TOURNOUR : Then he will be sitting up to finish his monthly abstracts, the accounts of the Master of Garrisowen Workhouse, bedad! (*There is a hint of mockery in in ' Master of Garrisowen Workhouse,' a tinge of emphasis in 'Accounts.'*)

CHRISTY : He goes out for a walk in the country these evenings. (*Tournour makes a leer of contempt.*) Do you never go out for a walk in the country, Felix Tournour?

TOURNOUR : They used to take me out for walks when I was a little fellow, but they never got me into the country since.

CHRISTY : I suppose, now you're in the porter's lodge, you watch everything that goes up and down the road?

TOURNOUR : It gratifies me to do so—would you believe that now?

CHRISTY : You know a lot, Felix Tournour.

TOURNOUR : We're told to advance in knowledge, young fellow. How long is Tom Muskerry the Master of Garrisowen Workhouse?

CHRISTY : Thirty years this spring.

TOURNOUR : There's where you're out. Twenty-nine years.

CHRISTY : Thirty years according to the abstracts here. And that's the full service.

TOURNOUR : Twenty-nine years.

CHRISTY : Thirty years.

TOURNOUR : Twenty-nine years. I was born in the Workhouse, and I mind when Tom Muskerry was pitchforked into it as our Master. We've been under him long enough. Whist now, here he is, and time for him.

> (*He falls into an officious manner. He closes up stove and puts bucket away, going L. He turns the gas on full.* CHRISTY CLARKE *rises and begins to arrange the newspapers on wooden chair. The corridor door opens. The man who appears is not the Master, however. He is a blind man dressed in pauper's garb.*)

CHRISTY : Myles Gorman.

> (MYLES GORMAN *is a Gael of the West of Ireland in whose face there is much intellectual vigour. He is about sixty and carries himself with energy. His face is pale and he has a fringe of white beard. The eyeballs in his head are contracted, but it is evident he has some vestige of sight. He advances into the room and stands there, turning to the two the attentive face of the blind.*)

GORMAN : Mister Muskerry! Are you there, Mister Muskerry?

TOURNOUR : What do you want, my oul' fellow?

GORMAN (*with a puzzled look*) : Well, now, I've a favour to ask of your honour.

TOURNOUR : Be off out of this to your ward.

GORMAN : Is that Mister Muskerry?

CHRISTY (*coming to* GORMAN'S *right*) : Mister Muskerry isn't here.

GORMAN : And who am I speaking to?

TOURNOUR : You're speaking to Felix Tournour from the Lodge, I'll have you know.

GORMAN : Felix Tournour! Aye, aye! Good evening, Felix Tournour. When will the Master be here?

TOURNOUR (*going to him*) : Not till you're out of this and back in your ward.

GORMAN : Wasn't there a boy speaking to me?

CHRISTY (*speaking as if to a deaf man*) : The Master will be going his rounds in a while, and you can speak to him in the ward.

GORMAN : I've a favour to ask the Master, and I don't want to ask it in front of the others. (*To* CHRISTY.) Will the Master be here soon, a vic vig?

TOURNOUR (*taking him by the shoulders*) : Here, now! This is your way out. (*He turns* GORMAN *to the door. As he is putting him out,* THOMAS MUSKERRY *enters.*)

TOURNOUR : This oul' fellow came into the office, and I was putting him back into his ward.

MUSKERRY : Leave the man alone.

> (TOURNOUR *retreats to the stove, and takes up the bucket: after a look behind, he goes out and closes the corridor door.* CHRISTY CLARKE *takes the newspapers over to the table and sits down.* MYLES GORMAN *remains eager and attentive.* THOMAS MUSKERRY *stands with his back to the stove. He is approaching seventy, a large man, fleshy in face and figure. Sanguine and benevolent in looks. He has the looks and movement of one in authority. His hair is white and long, his silver beard is trimmed, his clothes loosely fitting. He wears no overcoat but has a white knitted muffler round his neck. He has on a black, wide-brimmed hat, and carries a walking-stick.*)

MUSKERRY (*to* GORMAN) : Well, my good man?

GORMAN : I'm here to ask a favour from you, Master.

116

MUSKERRY : You should proffer your request when I'm in the ward. However, I am ready to give you my attention.

GORMAN : I'm a blinded man, Master, and when you're in the ward I can't get you by yourself conveniently. I can't come up to you like the other oul' men and speak to you private like.

MUSKERRY : Be that as it may, but now what would you have me do for you?

GORMAN (*eagerly*) : They tell me that to-morrow's market day, and I thought that you might give me a pass, and let me go out about the town.

MUSKERRY : We'll consider it, Gorman.

GORMAN : Master, let me out in the town on the market-day.

MUSKERRY : We couldn't let you out to play your pipes through the town.

GORMAN : I'm not thinking of the music at all, Master, but to be out in the day and to feel the throng, and to be talking to the men that do be on the roads.

MUSKERRY : We'll consider it, Gorman. (*He takes off the muffler and puts it on back of arm-chair.*)

GORMAN : Well, I'm very much obliged to your honour. (*He passes* MUSKERRY, *crossing R.* MUSKERRY *has been regarding him.*)

MUSKERRY : Tell me this, Gorman, were you always on the roads?

GORMAN : I wasn't brought up that way, because we'd a bit of land of our own. When I was driving cattle and I was dealing in horses. Then I took up with an oul' man and he taught me the pipes. I'm playing the pipes ever since and that's thirty years ago. Isn't it time my mission was ended, Master.

MUSKERRY : We come to an end, Gorman; we come to an end.

117

GORMAN : Well, the eyes began to wither up on me, and now I've only a stim of sight. I'm a blinded man from this out, Master.

MUSKERRY (*coming down to* GORMAN) : And what will you do?

GORMAN : Oh, sure the roads of Ireland are before me when I get my discharge from this; I'll be playing my bit of music. (*He goes towards the door.*)

MUSKERRY : Tell me: have you any family yourself?

GORMAN : Ne'er a chick nor child belonging to me. Ne'er a woman lay by me. I went the roads by myself. Will you think of what I asked you, Master?

MUSKERRY : I'll consider it.

GORMAN : Good-night to your honour. Remember my name, Master . . . Gorman, Myles Gorman.

(*He goes out.* MUSKERRY *stands looking after him.*)

MUSKERRY : Now, Christy Clarke, I consider that the man gone out is a very exceptional man.

CHRISTY (*standing up*) : Is it Myles Gorman?

MUSKERRY (*back at stove*) : Yes. I'd even say that, considering his station in life, Myles Gorman is a very superior man.

CHRISTY : They say he's not a good musician.

MUSKERRY : And maybe he's not. I consider, however, that there's great intelligence in his face. He stands before you, and you feel that he has the life of a young colt, and then you're bound to think that, in spite of the fact that he's blind and a wanderer, the man has not wasted his life. (MUSKERRY *settles himself in the arm-chair.*)

CHRISTY (*going to* MUSKERRY) : Will you give him leave to-morrow?

MUSKERRY : No, Christy, I will not.

CHRISTY : Why not, Mister Muskerry?

MUSKERRY : That man would break bounds and stay away.

CHRISTY : Do you think he would?

MUSKERRY : I know he would. He'd fly off like the wood-quest flying away from the tame pigeons.

CHRISTY : He and his brother had a farm between them. The day the brother told Myles to go to Dublin to see a comrade of his who was sick. Myles was home in a week. When he came back he found that his brother had sold the place and was gone out of the country.

MUSKERRY : His brother did wrong, but he didn't do so much wrong to Myles Gorman.

CHRISTY : How is that, Mister Muskerry?

MUSKERRY : He sent Myles Gorman to his own life. He's a man who went his own way always; a man who had never any family or affairs. A man, I'd have you know, Christy Clarke, far different from me. I was always in the middle of affairs. Then, too, I busied myself about other people. It was for the best, I think, but that's finished. On the desk is a letter that I want you to bring to me.

CHRISTY (going through papers) : " I am much obliged for your favour . . . "

MUSKERRY : That's not it.

CHRISTY (reading another paper) : " I am about to add to the obligations under which I stand to you, by recommending to your notice my grandson, Albert Crilly . . . "

MUSKERRY : That's the letter. It's the last of its kind. Bring it to me. (CHRISTY CLARKE brings the letter.) There comes a turn in the blood and a turn in the mind. I'm a thinking man, Christy ; I'd like to know the history of the parishes adjoining us—the well, the bushes, the old ruins. This while back, I've been going out to the country instead of into the town, and coming back here in the evenings I've seen the work-house with the big wall round it, and the big gate going into it, and I've said to myself that Thomas Muskerry ought to be as secure and contented here as if he was in his own castle.

CHRISTY : And so you ought, Mister Muskerry.

MUSKERRY : Look round at the office, Christy. I've made it as fit for me as the nest for the wren. I'll spend a few more years here, and then I'll go out on pension. I won't live in the town. I've seen a place in the country I'd like. Someone wrote about the big tree that's before its door.

CHRISTY : Maybe I know where it is.

MUSKERRY : I'll say no more about it now, but it's not far from this, and it's near the place where I was reared.

CHRISTY : And so you'll go back to your place?

MUSKERRY : As Oliver Goldsmith, my fellow countyman, and I might say, my fellow parishioner, says ... what's this the lines are about the hare, Christy?

CHRISTY : "And like the Hare whom Horns and Hounds pursue.
Pants to the place from whence at first he flew."

MUSKERRY : Aye. "And like the Hare whom Hounds and Horns pursue ... "

(*The clock strikes nine.*)

CHRISTY : You weren't on the rounds yet. Isn't that a strange ... ?

MUSKERRY (*startled*) : Would you believe it now, it was near passing my mind to go on my nightly rounds. What's come over me, Christy? (*He puts the letter in his pocket.*) Where's that fellow, Albert Crilly? He was to have been here to give me a hand with the abstracts. Christy Clarke, go down to Miss Coghlan's and get me two novelettes. Bring me back two nice love stories, and be here when I come back.

120

(Standing up, he puts on his scarf and possesses himself of the bunch of keys. CHRISTY CLARKE takes his cap off the rack and goes out. TOURNOUR enters, again with a bucket of coal. He takes it over to the stove.)

MUSKERRY : What have you there, Tournour?

TOURNOUR : Coal. It is to be remembered. Coal.

MUSKERRY : And sweep the office, Tournour. *(He goes out by the corridor door.)*

(The purposeful rattle TOURNOUR makes by opening and closing the stove and putting a shovel of coal in dissipates the quietude that MUSKERRY's attitude had produced. For the rest of the scene there is something excitable in the movements and speech of the characters. TOURNOUR takes sweeping-brush from under desk, L, and begins to sweep in direction of corridor door.)

TOURNOUR : Going for walks in the country, bedad! There's them in the town you've got enough of. You don't want to go bail for Madam Daughter, nor for Count Crofton Crilly, your son-in-law, nor for the Masters and Mistresses. All very well, my oul' gallavanter. That I may see them laying you out on the flags of hell!

(He puts the sweeping-brush upright and speaks to it.)

The Devil went out for a ramble at night,
Through Garrisowen Workhouse to see every sight.
The oul' men were dreaming of meat to come near
     them,
And the Devil cocked ears at the words for to hear
     them,
'Twice a year we get meat,' said the toothless oul'
     men,

121

' Oh, Lord send the meat won't be too tough again.
To clear away dishes Mick Fogarty goes,
May the Devil burn the nails off his toes.
Deep dreaming that night of fast days before,
Sagging the walls with the pull of his snore,
In his chamber above, Thomas Muskerry lay snug,
When the Devil this summons roared in his lug . . .

(*The door of the Master's apartment is opened, and*
ALBERT CRILLY *enters. He is a young man who might
be a bank clerk or a medical student. He is as much of
a dude as his means permit, but he also shows that he
has a certain wit and insight.*)

ALBERT (*lighting a cigarette*) : Is the grand-parent here,
Tournour?

TOURNOUR : He's gone on the Master's rounds, Mister
Albert. He rose from his bed late enough this morning.
He wasn't up in time to come to Mass with us.

ALBERT (*going to desk*) : There'll be trouble for the grand-
parent if that's noticed.

TOURNOUR : Oh, to be sure! And the nuns 'll notice it.

ALBERT : Well, he's near the end of his term here. But he
may have to give up soon.

TOURNOUR : He's well off that has somebody to do the
work for him. (*He continues to sweep towards corridor.*)

ALBERT : Tournour, you're a damned clever fellow. I
heard a piece of yours yesterday that I thought was
damned good.

TOURNOUR : Was it a rhyme?

ALBERT : Something about goings-on in the place we're in.

TOURNOUR (*as if giving himself the task of recollecting*) : Aye.
" The Devil's Rambles." Don't let the boss know and
I'll tell it to you.

(*He is about to begin the recitation when* CROFTON
CRILLY *enters from the Master's apartment.*

122

CROFTON CRILLY *is big and well made, has a fair beard.*
A pipe is always in his mouth. He is a loiterer, a
talker, a listener.)

CRILLY : I suppose your job is to finish the abstracts to-
night, Albert?

ALBERT : He's depending on me to finish them.

CRILLY : No leniency in the Local Government Board these
days. I'm told that . . .

ALBERT (*to the man with the sweeping-brush*) : Go on with
" The Devil's Rambles," Tournour.

CRILLY : I heard it in Keegan's. It's damn good.

TOURNOUR : I don't like saying it before Mister Crilly.

CRILLY : Go on with it, man. I'll leave a beer in Keegan's
for you.

TOURNOUR (*putting himself on terms with the others*) : Well,
you may reprimand me.

CRILLY : Have done talking, and go on with it.

TOURNOUR (*reciting*) :
In his chamber above . . . a person . . . lay snug,
When the Devil this summons roared in his lug—
' Get up,' said the Devil, ' and swear you'll be true,
And the oath of allegiance I'll tender anew.
You'll have pork, veal, and lamb, mutton-chops, fowl
and fish,
Cabbage and carrots and leeks as you wish,
No fast days to you will make visitation,
For your sake the town will have dispensation.
Long years you will have without envy or strife,
And when you depart you'll find the same life,
And in the next world you'll 've your will and your
sway,
With a poorhouse to govern all your own way,
And I'll promise you this: to keep up your state,
You'll have Felix Tournour to watch at the gate.'

CRILLY : That's damn good.

123

TOURNOUR : There's more of it, Mr. Crilly.

CRILLY : I must get a copy of the whole of it to show at Keegan's.

TOURNOUR : And I'll be obliged for what you'll leave me. (*He has swept as far as the corridor door. He opens it, goes out and closes door.*)

CRILLY : That's a clever fellow, a damn clever fellow, Albert. (*He goes to cabinet, takes out bottle and glass and pours himself a drink.*) They're getting rid of the billiard-marker at Keegan's.

ALBERT : Why's that?

CRILLY : Business going down. (*Standing at stove and emptying glass.*) Ah, this is a cursed town, Albert.

ALBERT : Every town in Ireland is a cursed town.

CRILLY : Ah, but this is an extraordinary cursed town. I could tell you something . . .

ALBERT : Covey?

CRILLY : Imagine that fellow Covey failing and getting out of the town!

ALBERT : Leaving thousands in debts, I presume.

CRILLY : I wouldn't put the figure that high, Albert.

ALBERT : What's it to you? You don't suspect that Covey stuck the grandfather?

CRILLY : Albert, your grandfather wouldn't back a bill for Pontius Pilate. Be said by your grandfather. Never back a bill, Albert.

ALBERT : Covey had the contract for the Workhouse coal.

CRILLY : He had that. He showed it to me. For supplying the Workhouse with a hundred tons of coal.

ALBERT : I hope the old man was in his right mind when dealing with Covey.

CRILLY : Albert, you don't know how these financial transactions work out. (*He roams about the office in a troubled way.*) If I had gone in for a government job at your age I'd have an independence now.

124

ALBERT : Independence?

CRILLY : I'd have a pension now. Well, the grandfather is looking after a job for you. It's wonderful the influence he has with high-up people.

ALBERT (*lighting a cigarette*) : What about the tailor in this town?

CRILLY : Tailor?

ALBERT : I'll want two new suits when I'm leaving this town.

CRILLY : Suits?

ALBERT : They'll have to be stylish! Smart! I'll be in a new set when I leave this town.

CRILLY : That'll cost money, Albert. And who has money in this place. (*Dismally.*) It's a blue lookout, Albert.

ALBERT : I'll be out of this before the change.

CRILLY : What change?

ALBERT : The grandfather will be retiring—maybe before the time he expects.

CRILLY : He'll be at home with us, you know, and I won't have a corner of the house for myself.

ALBERT : And mother has a man by the hand for grandfather's job.

CRILLY : James Scollard, eh? And I suppose I'll have him for a son-in-law. If Scollard gets the old man's job, he won't want Anna's money. It mightn't be a bad arrangement. And your mother will still have a hand in the affairs of the Workhouse.

ALBERT : It won't be the old business, I tell you, with Scollard. I have the letter that the old man has written for me here. (*He takes it up and reads it. And then goes back to work at the papers which he does in a proper clerky way.* CROFTON CRILLY *takes up a newspaper, seats himself in the arm-chair and relaxes even more. The clock ticks. In a distant ward a bell rings.*)

125

CRILLY (*letting his mind become engaged with new items*) :
Peter Macnabo! If I heard that name once I heard it
a hundred times! He was a friend of your grandfather's, but I'll go bail they didn't see each other
these forty years. Used to course hares or something.
The grandfather will be sorry to read this. Do you
know, Albert, there's no leniency anywhere nowadays.
Peter Macnabo, Master of the Workhouse in Dooard,
is having a Local Government Inquiry brought down
on him. He and your grandfather would be about the
same age, Albert.

ALBERT (*scrutinizing some papers*) : I don't know whether
the old man is crossing out figures or putting them in
here.

CRILLY : Incompetence! We're always hearing that word
now from these Local Government Board whipper-
snappers. Can't a man have any leeway these days, I
ask. Albert!

ALBERT (*gumming papers together*) : Well?

CRILLY : I'll take this paper, it's 'The Impartial Reporter,'
with me. The Master would be disheartened if he
read this account of his old crony. I'm all for letting
sleeping dogs lie.

ALBERT : I wouldn't let them lie too long.

CRILLY : You have some meaning in that, Albert.

ALBERT : I have. (*He takes the paper from* CRILLY.) I'll put
a blue pencil mark, round the item and leave it for
the grandfather.

CRILLY : You don't know, Albert, how these—what you
might call parallelisms—dishearten a man.

ALBERT : It might be like a summons in the grandfather's
case—getting to be careful.

CRILLY : Is he not, Albert?

ALBERT : Not from what I see before me. (*He turns from
desk and lights a cigarette.*)

126

CRILLY : And so you've finished the abstracts for him?

ALBERT : As far as I can go. The stores—the accounts for the stores—will take another bit of my time.

CRILLY : The stores, Albert?

ALBERT : There's where Covey's cuteness and the grand-parent's simpleness come together. I'll put this where he'll take notice. (*Having marked the paper he puts it down.*)

CRILLY : Covey! Don't mention that man's name again, Albert! And intruding here, too!

ALBERT : Coming up to the office here, to the storehouse here! And there are sharp eyes in the porter's lodge.

CRILLY : The Devil's Rambles, Albert.

ALBERT (*ready to leave the office*) : I see a draft of that letter of recommendation. I suppose he'll put it in a clear hand.

CRILLY : He'll give it to your mother, Albert.

(THOMAS MUSKERRY *enters. He nods to* CROFTON CRILLY *and addresses* ALBERT.)

MUSKERRY : Is all finished?

ALBERT : The abstracts are, and you can get them off. I'll come in again to deal with the stores.

MUSKERRY : And your letter will be ready then.

ALBERT : Thanks, Grandpa.

CRILLY (*effusively*) : You have the utmost of our thanks.

MUSKERRY : And now I'll settle down to myself.

(CROFTON CRILLY *and* ALBERT *go out.* MUSKERRY *makes himself comfortable for the hours of the night when he will be on easy duty. He takes muffler off. He puts shawl round his shoulders. He brings the arm-chair nearer the stove. He sees the marked newspaper that* ALBERT CRILLY *has left for him, takes it up and reads.*)

127

MUSKERRY : "Dooard Workhouse. Local Government Board intervenes. Enquiry to be made." Marked! That's no way to bring this to my notice. And so at the end of it all they're inquiring into your competence, Peter Macnabo! And we two the last of our generation of officials. But is this a way to bring that to my notice?

(CHRISTY CLARKE *enters.*)

MUSKERRY : Wasn't he glad to mark it with his blue pencil, the impudent puppy, with his tongue in his cheek!

CHRISTY : Mister Muskerry?

MUSKERRY (*mildly*) : Well, Christy?

CHRISTY : Aren't you well in your thirty years here as Master?

MUSKERRY : And what of that?

CHRISTY : I heard a man say that there isn't a Workhouse Master in Ireland that has so long a service.

MUSKERRY : The length of service isn't everything. It's the beneficialness of the service. And I'd make bold to say, Christy Clarke, that it was beneficial. No one that comes after me can have the same heart for the poor that I have. I was earning in the year of the famine. I saw able men struggling to get work that would give them a handful of Indian meal. And I saw little children waiting on the road for some relief! That's why no one that comes after me can be as good a Master of Garrisowen Workhouse as I am.

CHRISTY (*heartily*) : That's known, Mister Muskerry.

MUSKERRY : Boards! Local Government Boards! They're going to make out that my old friend, Peter Macnabo, is incompetent to manage Dooard Workhouse.

(CHRISTY *holds out to him a bunch of keys.*)

MUSKERRY : Didn't I hang them up there, Christy, when I came in? It's hard to believe that I'd ever leave them behind.

(CHRISTY *hangs the bunch in its place.*)
Bring me a little whiskey, Christy.

(CHRISTY *opens the cabinet and takes out bottle.*)

CHRISTY : There isn't any in the bottle, Mister Muskerry.

MUSKERRY (*with resentment*) : No. I suppose not. And that puppy, Albert Crilly, had the impertinence, the damned, confounded impertinence, to leave this paper for me with the belittlement of my old friend, Peter Macnabo, marked with his blue pencil.

CHRISTY : There's the novelette. Miss Coghlan says it's a nice love story. " The Heart of Angelina" it is called.

MUSKERRY : It will take my mind off the badness of the world. (*He settles himself in his chair.*) Good-night, Christy.

CHRISTY : Good-night, Mister Muskerry. (*He goes out.*)

MUSKERRY : " The Heart of Angelina." Of all the infernal puppies!

(*The curtain falls to mark a passage of time.*)

ACT ONE, SCENE TWO

(*The same office. The time is the later part of the second evening after the closing of the scene. The gas is lighted.* ALBERT CRILLY *is at desk, working at papers.* ANNA CRILLY *enters. She is twenty: good-looking, self-possessed.*)

ANNA : Are you working on grandfather's accounts, Albert?

ALBERT : You can see that I am. For the Audit Department of the Local Government Board. And if I didn't put my time on them, the Audit Department would be here in double-quick time to put the grandad through his paces.

ANNA : Mister Scollard was speaking to a man from the Audit Department. (*Everything she says is cool and deliberate, but her voice is neither cold nor sharp*).

ALBERT : Ah, your James Scollard, the old man's would-be successor.

ANNA : We won't go into that, Albert.

ALBERT : He's very watchful for us all, isn't he?

ANNA : There's no one as wide-awake in the town, Albert. He heard that the porter in the lodge . . .

ALBERT : The Devil's Rambles!

ANNA : Speak sensibly, Albert.

ALBERT : Well, Felix Tournour. What about him?

ANNA : He was drinking in Keegan's last night, and he said something about the stores that are in grand-father's charge.

ALBERT : He has sharp eyes—damn sharp eyes.
    The Devil went out for a ramble one night,
    Through Garrisowen Workhouse to see every sight.

130

ANNA : That's very vulgar, Albert. Mister Scollard wants
you to take a lot of care in the way you bring things
forward:

ALBERT : He's an interfering fellow, Scollard.

ANNA : What Mister Scollard is doing is for our good.

ALBERT : The good of the Crillys, eh?

> (MRS. CRILLY *enters. She is a woman around forty
> with a watchful expression that impairs the remains
> of her good looks.*)

MRS. CRILLY (*closing the door carefully*) : Is he still on his
rounds?

ALBERT : Well, he's not here.

MRS. CRILLY : Have you anything to tell us, Albert?

ALBERT (*turning from the desk and addressing the two women
with some authority*) : You know that for a while back
I've thought that grandfather was failing. Coming
here to give him a hand with abstracts and accounts I
saw signs of that. That young fellow, Christy Clarke,
has been doing a few things that saved him a bit in the
wear and tear of office work. What I did for him
myself . . .

MRS. CRILLY (*taking from his air of authority*) : Your grandfather's got the job for you, Albert.

ALBERT : That's right. Well, considering his age . . .

ANNA : What's Albert telling us, Mother?

MRS. CRILLY : I think I know.

ALBERT : But it would have been all right only that fellow,
Covey, came along . . .

MRS. CRILLY : He had a contract with the Workhouse . . .

ALBERT : To supply tons of coal.

MRS. CRILLY : The Guardians paid him . . .

ALBERT : For forty tons of coal on the certificate that the
grandfather signed.

MRS. CRILLY : I want to hear what else.

ALBERT : I didn't know it was as much as forty tons, but here's the certificate with as good a signature of the grandfather's as ever I've looked at. But if anybody looked over the stores, what would he see? Ten tons or thereabouts. Well, then, the grandfather certified for forty tons instead of what the Workhouse got, twenty tons, or else he has allowed twenty tons to be stolen from the stores.

MRS. CRILLY : What are you going to do, Albert?

ALBERT : I'll leave a note here for him. I'm not going to be the informer.

MRS. CRILLY : He'll have to resign before this comes out.

ALBERT : Before the Local Government Board gets wind of it.
  (*Lighting a cigarette,* ALBERT *goes out.*)

MRS. CRILLY : If he resigns now his pension is safe. There is nothing else against him.

ANNA : Oh, he'll have to have his pension. Mother, hasn't grandfather two hundred pounds invested in the shop?

MRS. CRILLY : It's not a definite sum. It wouldn't be called an investment.

ANNA : Mother, is my money safe?

MRS. CRILLY : Yes, Anna. But if we help James Scollard to get the Master's place . . .

ANNA : Whether Mister Scollard gets the place or does not get it, I'll want all my money.

MRS. CRILLY : Don't press me now, Anna. I've so much to think about . . . If he resigned now, a new Master would be soon appointed. The deficiency in the stores would not be noticed until he came in.

ANNA : The new Master? But would he pass such a thing, Mother?

MRS. CRILLY : It's a question of your grandfather having to hand back all that money after he had retired. What have we all been planning for? For your James Scollard to succeed your grandfather.

132

ANNA (*her hand on door-handle*) : And that's what I go to James Scollard with!

MRS. CRILLY (*with great earnestness*) : You know how we are situated, Anna.

(*The door is opened and* THOMAS MUSKERRY *enters.*)

MUSKERRY (*pleased with the sight of her*) : Well, Nancy.

ANNA : Good evening, Grandpapa.

MRS. CRILLY : Good evening, Father.

MUSKERRY (*coming in to office and taking off his scarf*) : This Nancy girl is looking remarkably well. (*To* MRS. CRILLY.) Well, Marianne, and how are you? I have written the letter that will get the situation for that rascally Albert.

MRS. CRILLY : You are very good.

MUSKERRY : In season and out of season I've put myself at your service. I can do no more for ye. (*He sits down and speaks in a reconciling tone.*) You're looking well, Marianne.

MRS. CRILLY : I'm beginning to feel well again.

MUSKERRY : And the infant? What age is he now?

MRS. CRILLY : Little Joseph is ten months old.

MUSKERRY : I dreamt of him last night. I thought Joseph became a bishop. He ought to be reared for the Church, Marianne. Well, well, I've nothing more to do with that. Did Christy Clarke bring me any reading matter?

ANNA : Christy Clarke hasn't been here at all, Grandfather.

MUSKERRY : Stand, till I look at you, Nancy. (*He looks her over with approval as she stands in the light.*) I wouldn't be surprised if you were the best-looking girl in the town, Nancy.

ANNA (*without coquettishness*) : Anna Crilly is not going into competition with the others. (*She unwraps his muffler and kisses him.*) Good night, Grandpapa. (*She goes out by the corridor door.*)

133

(THOMAS MUSKERRY *goes to the desk, takes up a letter, and hands it to* MRS. CRILLY *with a sort of stateliness.*)

MRS. CRILLY : The letter for Albert?

MUSKERRY : I think, Marianne, it's the last thing I can do for you or yours.

MRS. CRILLY : Well, we can't tell a bad story of you. We want you to come to dinner on Sunday. I've been able to get a lamb out of Ginnell's field.

MUSKERRY (*interested*) : What sort is the lamb?

MRS. CRILLY : Oh, a very young lamb. Anna will make the gooseberry tart you like.

MUSKERRY : I'll send round a bottle of wine. Perhaps we'll be in the way of celebrating something for Albert.

MRS. CRILLY : Nancy was saying that you might like to stay a few days with us.

MUSKERRY : Stay a few days! How could I do that, ma'am?

MRS. CRILLY : You could get someone to look after the house. James Scollard would do it, and you could stay with us for a few days.

MUSKERRY : Well, indeed, I'll do no such thing. What put it in your head to ask me this?

MRS. CRILLY : Nancy said . . .

MUSKERRY : Let the girl speak for herself. What's in your mind, Marianne?

MRS. CRILLY : Maybe I went at it wrongly. You're not looking well, Father.

MUSKERRY : I'm as well as ever I was.

MRS. CRILLY : Others do not think so.

MUSKERRY : I suppose it's got around that I was late a few mornings. No matter for that. I'm as well as ever I was. No more talk about it. And there's work I have to do between this and my bed-time. (*He goes over to desk.* MRS. CRILLY *watches him carefully.*)

134

(FELIX TOURNOUR *comes in with a bucket. He goes to stove. He bangs the door of the stove as he opens it and rattles a poker within. He has the centre of the scene.*)

MUSKERRY (*sharply*) : What are you doing there, Tournour?

TOURNOUR : Coals, I'll have you know, Mister Muskerry.
   (*He contrives to make his bearing menacing and his speech insolent.*)

MUSKERRY : I don't want all that disturbance while I'm here.

TOURNOUR : While you're here, is it, Mister Muskerry?

MUSKERRY : I told you, and you can go.

TOURNOUR (*looking into the bucket*) : There's still coals, Mister Muskerry.

MUSKERRY : That will do. Good night, Tournour.

TOURNOUR : Good-night, Mister Muskerry. (*Bucket in his hand,* TOURNOUR *goes out.* MUSKERRY *takes up the note that* ALBERT *left. He reads*):

MUSKERRY : " You certified for forty tons of coal delivered. It appears that Covey put in only twenty." (*perturbed*). Who left this here?

MRS. CRILLY : Albert left it for you.

MUSKERRY : The impudent rascal! How dare he address himself like that to me?

MRS. CRILLY : He was making the accounts ready . . .

MUSKERRY : That much was owed to me.

MRS. CRILLY : He saw your certificate there and he knew . . .

MUSKERRY : What ma'am?

MRS. CRILLY : It was for eighty tons and only forty were delivered.

MUSKERRY : It's a lie, and a damn infernal lie. I was in the stores the other day and I saw what coals were there. Certainly forty tons had been taken out of it. There was . . . (*He stands looking out. He realized that what he saw was not nearly the quantity of what should have been there. Suddenly he becomes a helpless man.*)

135

MUSKERRY : Marianne!

MRS. CRILLY : Well, Father.

MUSKERRY : Peter Macnabo . . .

MRS. CRILLY : Who?

MUSKERRY : You might remember him, for he and I were a good deal together. And now there's to be an Inquiry about him.

MRS. CRILLY : They had nothing against you before this.

MUSKERRY : I was spoken of as the pattern for the officials of Ireland.

MRS. CRILLY : If you resigned now . . .

MUSKERRY : Before this came out . . . Marianne, it would be like the blow to the struck ox if I lost my pension.

MRS. CRILLY : It could be made secure. And we could pay back to the Guardians by instalments.

MUSKERRY : If I resigned now where would I go to?

MRS. CRILLY : It was always understood that you would stay with us.

MUSKERRY : No, Marianne.

MRS. CRILLY : You'll have the place to yourself. Albert will be away. The boys will be going to school. Anna could do things for you.

MUSKERRY : It is not what I was looking to.

MRS. CRILLY : Oh, well, if you have a better place to go to . . .

MUSKERRY : Remember what I said, Marianne, I've worked for you and yours, in season and out of season. There should be no more claims on me.

MRS. CRILLY : There are no more claims on you.

MUSKERRY : I am willing to leave in the shop what I put into the shop. Let Anna know that it will come to her from me. I'll write to the Guardians tonight, and send in my resignation. I venture to think they will know their loss.

MRS. CRILLY : They will. (*She goes out quietly.*)

136

MUSKERRY (*looking round the office*) : And I had made this place as fit for me as the nest of the wren. (*with sudden resentment.*) Wasn't he glad to write that note, the impudent rascal, with his tongue in his cheek! There's the other place that I'll go to after a while.

(CHRISTY CLARKE *comes in by the corridor door with magazines.*)

MUSKERRY : They want me to resign from this place, Christy.

CHRISTY : Not be Master of Garrisowen Workhouse?

MUSKERRY : I'm a long time here, Christy, a long time.

CHRISTY (*with regret*) : I suppose that's the case, Misrer Muskerry.

MUSKERRY : And it has been shown to me, Christy, that I'm at my failing time.

(*A bell is heard tolling.*)

What's that for, Christy?

CHRISTY : Malachi O'Rourke, the Prince, as they used to call him, is dead.

MUSKERRY : Aye, I gave orders to toll him when he died. He was here for a long time, a pauper, but he was an estated gentleman, and songs were made about his family. There were people who used to annoy him, but he's gone from them now.

CHRISTY : Miss Coghlan picked two nice love-stories for you.

MUSKERRY : I haven't the heart to read, Christy.

CHRISTY : Good-night, Mister Muskerry.

MUSKERRY : Good-night, my boy.

(*He stands with his hands on the back of the arm-chair. The bell tolls.*)

CURTAIN

137

ACT TWO

Scene: The yard outside the Workhouse. Low walls right and left, a gate in wall right. Back is part of wall of the Workhouse, a few steps before it. There is a bench back left : two old men are seated on it.

FIRST OLD MAN (*with vague reflectiveness*) : Lima, the capital of Peru, is six thousand feet above the sea level.

SECOND MAN : Don't be giving us any of your book-learning. Have you a bit of tobacco?

FIRST OLD MAN : Nary bit.

>   (CROFTON CRILLY *and* JAMES SCOLLARD *come in through gate,* SCOLLARD *carrying a satchel.*)

CRILLY : You're sure of the votes, James. We'll give the Guardians a few minutes to get into the Board Room.

SCOLLARD : May I ask, Mister Crilly . . .

CRILLY (*laying his hand on* SCOLLARD'S *shoulder*) : Not a word, James. It's all as good as settled. Doherty isn't in the running. He has no influence.

SCOLLARD : My character, my record . . .

CRILLY : Influence! I've seen to it that you have it, James. It might look better if I didn't vote for you.

SCOLLARD : But, Mister Crilly . . .

CRILLY : Prospective father-in-law! But you're well fixed without my vote. Doherty isn't in it. Make your mind easy about that! I'd give something, James, to be as secure as you are this day.

SCOLLARD (*feeling something anxious in his tone*) : The shop? I mean, I'd like to know . . .

CRILLY : Ah, don't be talking, man. We're doing the best we can for you. You know that, James.

SCOLLARD : No doubt you are, Mister Crilly.

138

CRILLY : You don't know how lucky you are, James Scollard. If there was somebody the like of me could get a backing from!

SCOLLARD : I'm well fitted for the place.

CRILLY : There's no one but will say you know the place in and out. But, good God! When I think of you in the place of the man that's leaving . . . Well, that was the Master!

SCOLLARD : He had excellent qualities—no one will deny that. But we're coming into a time when statistics are in the field.

CRILLY : Statistics! Running a workhouse with statistics!

SCOLLARD : I don't say that. But a person in charge of a workhouse will have to know about the itinerant in relation to the normally productive, the ratio of disablement . . .

CRILLY : Don't say a word about it to the Guardians, James! We'll turn in now.

(*They go through the gate.*)

FIRST OLD MAN : He'll be leaving to-day.

SECOND OLD MAN : Who'll be leaving? Tell me who'll be leaving this bloody oul' Workhouse?

FIRST OLD MAN : The Master that was—Mr. Muskerry.

SECOND OLD MAN : I'm twenty years here and he never left it before. Is he going to take the salt-water? Officiated people like to be at the seaside with the breezes and the high waves.

FIRST OLD MAN : That's what they call vacation. That's not why he's going. (*Speaking as if to a deaf man.*) He's leaving. Retiring. Going on a pension.

SECOND OLD MAN : Will there be a new Master? Or will it be the nuns that will be keeping the place?

FIRST OLD MAN : How would they know how to keep the place? There has to be a head to a workhouse the same as there has to be a head to a government.

139

SECOND OLD MAN : There will be a new Master. I didn't think I'd live to see a new Master in Garrisowen Workhouse.

FIRST OLD MAN : It will be all the same. We'll be paupers still.

SECOND OLD MAN : What did you say?

FIRST OLD MAN : We'll be paupers still.

SECOND OLD MAN : Nary bit of tobacco!

FIRST OLD MAN : Nary full breakfast of tea and bread and butter!

SECOND OLD MAN : Stirabout!

FIRST OLD MAN : If I had my flute I could play that tune over for you. "The bells they did ring and the stirabout did appear."

> (THOMAS MUSKERRY *comes on the steps. He is dressed in a way that is dignified and striking.* FELIX TOURNOUR *comes in by the gate.*)

MUSKERRY (*looking across the wall to his left from the steps*) : The bed of lettuce that I planted! It has grown well. I'm the owner of it—no one else.

TOURNOUR (*putting himself in a position where he can chaff* MUSKERRY) : Going abroad in your half-tall hat!

MUSKERRY (*resenting his insolence*) : Tournour!

TOURNOUR (*with change of tone*) : All outfitted for departure. I meant to say.

MUSKERRY : I'm Master here, Tournour.

TOURNOUR (*astonished*) : Master!

MUSKERRY : Until I'm given word that a new Master has been appointed by the Board of Guardians.

TOURNOUR : So that's how it is! The Master! As it was in the beginning now and ever shall be . . . Amen!

> (*He turns away.*)

MUSKERRY : The scoundrel! The damn scoundrel . . . ! The damn infernal scoundrel!

FIRST PAUPER : Mister Muskerry.

MUSKERRY : You, Cripes. What can I do for you?

FIRST PAUPER : Isn't this the day you're leaving the Workhouse, sir—this day of all days?

(*His saying this brings realization to* MUSKERRY. *He looks around.*)

MUSKERRY : I suppose that's what you had to talk about at your breakfast this morning and at your supper last night! The day of his Mastership over! Thomas Muskerry leaving Garrisowen Workhouse!

SECOND PAUPER : Oh, you're well out of it, Mister Muskerry! Many of the oul' men were saying that!

MUSKERRY : You wouldn't know. You never had sway over anything!

FIRST PAUPER : Nabuchanessare, King of the Jews,
An old pair of stockings and a new pair of shoes!

SECOND PAUPER : A new pair of shoes, bedad!

MUSKERRY : Well out of it! Had the inmates no more to say of me than that?

FIRST PAUPER : Oh, there was more than that, Mister Muskerry.

MUSKERRY : What was it?

FIRST PAUPER : I disremember.

SECOND PAUPER : You're well out of it, Mister Muskerry. What's a workhouse?

FIRST PAUPER : Ay, indeed. What's a workhouse? And what do they be thinking of in a workhouse—the oul' men, I mean—but a bit of tobacco?

MUSKERRY : I saw to it that they got their tobacco.

SECOND PAUPER : There ought to be a bit over and above the allowance. Send us a bit now and then, Mister Muskerry, and we won't forget you.

MUSKERRY : They expect me to have some care for them. I'll be in and out to them. And there's the lettuce.

(CHRISTY CLARKE *comes through the gate.*)

141

CHRISTY : Well, Mister Muskerry!

MUSKERRY : So you've come, Christy . . . It's early yet.

CHRISTY : It is, if you're not wanting to get away.

MUSKERRY : I'll be leaving behind me . . . I was forty years
here, Christy! A lot's left behind in one way or
another. I may be sending you back here now and
again. There's a good bed of lettuce here, and you
could get me a head as I wanted it.

CHRISTY : Will they let me . . . ?

MUSKERRY : Why wouldn't they? It was me that planted
them. (CHRISTY *assents*). The old men there . . .
they'll be expecting me keep an interest in them.

CHRISTY : They'll be sorry for the change, Mister
Muskerry.

MUSKERRY : And it will be a change! Believe you me,
Christy, it will be a change. When I walk out there
and through the gate by the roadside it will be the
same as if a history was ended. Do you know, Christy,
when I came here there were old men in the wards
who had stood before Daniel O'Connell at Mullagha-
mast. They came from different parts to hear him
that day. 'Forty of us slept in the one bed,' one of
them said to me—'a ploughed field.' That was
history. And when I go out of the gate there will be
something different here. Old Ireland will have gone
out of it. . . . And so you've come to take away my
belongings, Christy?

CHRISTY : When it's time, Mister Muskerry.

MUSKERRY : As for the belongings of mine that are left,
they are all in a portmanteau—

    (CROFTON CRILLY *with* JAMES SCOLLARD *comes to
them.*)

CRILLY : Come along, James. (*To* MUSKERRY). All's over
but the shouting.

MUSKERRY (*testily*) : And what do you mean by that, sir?

CRILLY : There was a faction . . . Well, to make a long story short, James Scollard's in.

SCOLLARD : Your unworthy successor, Mister Muskerry.

MUSKERRY : It's not for us to say that, Mister Scollard.

CRILLY : It's for the Board of Guardians, James. And they know, and I know, and you know you'll have to put a lot of good work in before they'll say of you what they said about your predecessor.

MUSKERRY : And what was that, may I ask?

SCOLLARD : They said I was following on one who was the pattern for the officials of Ireland.

CRILLY : And there wasn't one of them but agreed with that!

MUSKERRY : May be there was a motion to enter that on the minutes of the meeting.

CRILLY : Was there, James?

SCOLLARD : I believe that was done.

MUSKERRY : And now, sir, if you'll be good enough to come with me, I'll take you to the office and show you the books and the keys.

(*He turns to the building:* SCOLLARD *goes with him into the door above the steps.*)

CRILLY (*fuming*) : And damn little thanks I've got from that fellow, Scollard! I don't believe he'd ask me into Keegan's for a mouth-warmer. Well, Marianne will be pleased, and that will make things easier all round. I'm damned if I know how to break it to her if that Covey fellow turns his back on me. (*Turns to* CHRISTY). You were always a help to the old man— I mean the Master—I mean Mister Muskerry, my father-in-law.

CHRISTY : And when he goes to the house in the country——

CRILLY : What did you say?

CHRISTY : When he goes to his house in the country my mother will look after him.

143

CRILLY : Yes. Some time later. He'll be with us for a while. Then into real retirement with his pension, under his own vine and fig leaf. I wish I were in his shoes. God knows I do!

(FELIX TOURNOUR *comes out of the door above the steps carrying a very worn portmanteau.*)

TOURNOUR (*to* CHRISTY) : I've saved you that much labour. There's a hand barrow for you to wheel it in.

CRILLY : So you don't feel inclined to finish what you began, Tournour? Ah, there's too many like that in this town!

TOURNOUR (*making a gesture with his arms*) : Me push a barrow down the street in Garrisowen! Me, the Ward Master!

CRILLY : You're the gate-keeper, Tournour.

TOURNOUR : Do you say so? But doesn't a gate-keeper know what's coming in through the gate, and doesn't that help him to promotion? Sure it does, and you know it, Mister Crilly. You're a guardian, and you know that much.

CRILLY (*realizing that there is a threat in* TOURNOUR'S *look*) : Now, now, Tournour! Your manner . . .

TOURNOUR : Oh, my manner is it, Mister Crilly?

CRILLY : Well, I'm sure . . . Well, Christy Clarke won't mind doing it. Anything for the Master . . .

TOURNOUR : The Master that's going to give me promotion is Mister James Scollard, and you know why, Mr. Crilly. The gate-keeper is a likely man for the post of Ward Master.

CRILLY : Was there ever a town that was so full of villains! (*A man carrying an antique camera with its trivet and black cloth enters through the gate. He has a beard and sharp eyes behind spectacles.*)

144

PHOTOGRAPHER (*to* CRILLY) : I'm not mistaken, am I, in figuring that an important event is taking place here to-day? (*Leaving down the apparatus he takes a professional look at the yard and the persons.*) Confirmations, Confraternity Meetings, Ordinations, Weddings— I record them in my own special manner. Single photograph one shilling and sixpence, group two shillings and sixpence. I am Bartholomew Vincent Murann, Photographer to the Maharajah of Judpur.

CRILLY : That's a long way off.

MURANN : I travel. Recently I was where His Highness and suite were on a liner bound for the United States. They stepped on Irish ground. He gave me his patronage then. (*Turning to* CRILLY *with an album.*) You'll find the photographs there, sir. (CRILLY *takes album.*) I thought I might take the photograph here before the assembling of the First Communion class.

CRILLY : What photograph?

MURANN : The new Master of the Workhouse.

CRILLY : 'Pon my word, you fellows are ready for the drop kick! He has only been appointed.

MURANN : First day in office! Something to show in the parlour in after years! Ah, what a wonderful thing is the camera! What it can hand down to posterity!— And so reasonable in price!

TOURNOUR : I'll get my own likeness taken at the reasonable price of one and sixpence.

CRILLY : A picture of Tournour, no less!

TOURNOUR : To put in the Ward Master's office.

CRILLY : Office?

TOURNOUR : If there isn't an office, I'll get one.

CRILLY (*in disgust*) : Give him the Workhouse!

MURANN : What a picturesque nook this is! A setting indeed! The grey old walls! The massive doorway! Something that's like . . . Well, well, who knows what it's like? If there was some figure there!

(THOMAS MUSKERRY *comes on the steps.*) By Jove, that's it! That's it! The Master!

CRILLY : Not the Master you want.

MURANN (*to* MUSKERRY) : Stay, sir! Don't move!

(MUSKERRY *in astonishment keeps his position.*)

CRILLY : He's retired—he's not Master any more.

MURANN : He's the proper figure for the Master, standing there! Oh, sir, would you keep your stand just for a minute. A photograph of you is required!

(*He sets up his apparatus.*)

MUSKERRY : May I ask who you are, sir?

MURANN : Bartholomew Vincent Murann, photographer at large.

MUSKERRY : Has this been ordered?

(*The photographer is now busy getting black cloth over his head and the camera.*)

MUSKERRY : The Guardians aren't as neglectful as I thought.

TOURNOUR : At one-and-sixpence to you, Mister Muskerry.

(MUSKERRY *notices him but says nothing.* CRILLY *opens the album that had been given him.*)

MURANN : The Maharajah and his suite. And passengers from our port on the gangway.

CRILLY : Passengers! I'd like to see myself amongst them!

MURANN : Splendid position! Just a little to the right. I'll have you dominate the prospect.

(*Under the black cloth there are hurried movements.* CHRISTY CLARKE *enters wheeling a barrow.* CRILLY *finds something in the album that startles him.*)

CRILLY : God in Heaven! What am I looking at? It isn't Covey! On the gangway of a liner for America! If that's him, it will be the end of me!

(*The photographer comes from under the black cloth.*)

146

MURANN : I'm proud, sir, proud of having the opportunity
of obtaining such a striking photograph. It will be
looked on as a work of art. There you are, a majestic
figure, if I may say so, with the wall of the establishment you officiated in at your back. A worthy
memento this will be!

MUSKERRY : The Board of Guardians can put under it what
was publically stated—" The pattern of the officials
of Ireland."

TOURNOUR : Maybe they will and maybe they won't.

MUSKERRY (*coming to him*) : Tournour!

TOURNOUR : Humbly asking the pardon of the retired
Master of Garrisowen Workhouse! !

(CHRISTY CLARKE *enters with barrow.*)

CHRISTY : I'm ready to take your portmanteau now, Mr.
Muskerry.

MUSKERRY : You're a very willing lad, Christy. But
Tournour is here.

TOURNOUR : I carried the portmanteau out for you.

MUSKERRY : I see that, Tournour. And now will you take
it further—to Mister Crilly's—in the barrow.

TOURNOUR : That's the boy's job. I don't want to be wheeling a barrow down the street.

MUSKERRY : You're an attendant in the Workhouse,
Tournour, and the boy isn't. It is by an attendant in the
Workhouse that my baggage is to be taken out of the
Workhouse.

TOURNOUR : The boy can do it.

MUSKERRY : I've told you what to do, Tournour.

(TOURNOUR, *sullenly, puts the portmanteau on the
barrow and wheels it through the gate. The photographer is engaged with his apparatus.* CROFTON
CRILLY *on the bench is in a state of collapse.* THOMAS
MUSKERRY *stands looking at the side of the workhouse
that is before him.*)

147

MUSKERRY : There's where I was Master, Christy. Well, well, I'm my own man now.

CHRISTY : That's a great thing to be able to say.

MUSKERRY : If there's anything to be said against me, I'll hear it.

CRILLY : (*coming out of his torpor*) : Against you? Who's saying it?

MUSKERRY : I'll be with you, Crofton. A sojourner.

(*The photographer gives* MUSKERRY *a card.* JAMES SCOLLARD *comes on the steps that* MUSKERRY *had been on.*)

MURANN : The new Master, I presume. Stand there, if you please.

SCOLLARD (*to* CRILLY) : Should I let him detain me?

CRILLY : Oh, to Hell with photographing, anyway.

MURANN : (*to* SCOLLARD) : Just as you are.

(*As* MUSKERRY *with* CHRISTY *goes to the gate, a pauper comes to him.*)

PAUPER : Don't forget us, Mister Muskerry.

MUSKERRY : I won't, Cripes. (*To* CHRISTY). They're the old timers. They'll see me from time to time.

(*He and* CHRISTY *go out of gate.* CROFTON CRILLY *shrugs his shoulders and follows them despondently. With the black cloth over the camera and his head the photographer occupies centre while* JAMES SCOLLARD *remains on steps.*)

CURTAIN

148

ACT THREE

A month later. In Crilly's. The room is a parlour off the shop. A glass door, right, leads into the shop, and the fire-place is above this door. In the back, right, is a cupboard door. Back is a window looking on the street. A door, left, leads to other rooms. There is a table near the shop door and a horse-hair sofa back, an arm-chair at the fire, and two leather-covered chairs about. Conventional pictures on walls, and two certificates framed.

It is the forenoon of an April day. MRS. CRILLY is seated on the sofa, going through a heap of account books. ANNA CRILLY is at window. CROFTON CRILLY enters from shop.

CRILLY : It's all right, Marianne.

MRS. CRILLY : Well?

CRILLY : The Guardians insisted on appointing an outside person to take stock in the Workhouse stores. It's the new regulations, you know. Well, the job lay between young Dobbs and Albert . . .

MRS. CRILLY : You say it's all right?

CRILLY : Albert's got it.

MRS. CRILLY : I hope Albert will know what to do.

CRILLY : Oh, he'll know all right. Where's the Master?

MRS. CRILLY : He's in his room upstairs.

CRILLY : Was he not out this morning?

MRS. CRILLY : He's not dressed yet.

CRILLY : He was more particular when he was in his office

MRS. CRILLY : I daresay.

ANNA (*at window*) : I know whose those two children now. They are the new gas-manager's children.

CRILLY : He's a Scotchman.

149

ANNA : And married for the second time. Mother, Mrs. Dunne is going to the races. Such a sketch of a hat!

MRS. CRILLY (*gathering up her account books*) : It would be better for her if she stayed at home and looked after the business.

ANNA : She won't have much business to look after soon. That's the third time her husband has come out of Farrell's public-house.

CRILLY : He's drinking with the Dispensary Doctor. Companions! They're the curse of this town, Marianne. (*He sits down.*)

ANNA : She's walked into a blind man, hat and all. He's from the Workhouse.

CRILLY : He's the blind piper out of the Workhouse. Myles Gorman.

MRS. CRILLY (*to* ANNA) : You should go into the shop, Anna. Mary's not there.

ANNA : Yes, Mother. (*She crosses.*) James Scollard is coming in, Mother.

MRS. CRILLY : Very well, Anna. Stay in the shop.

(ANNA *goes into the shop.* CRILLY *moves about.*)

MRS. CRILLY : You're very uneasy.

CRILLY : Yes. I am uneasy, Marianne. There's some presentment on me. Eighty pounds a year is a good pension for the old man. He's a month out now. He ought to be getting his allowance.

(ANNA *comes from shop.*)

ANNA : Mother, the Surveyor's daughter is in the shop.

MRS. CRILLY : What does she want?

ANNA (*imitating an accent*) : Send up a pound of butter, two pounds of sugar, a pound of tea.

MRS. CRILLY : These people are paying nobody. But we can't refuse her. I suppose we'll send them up. But be very distant with her, Anna.

ANNA : I've kept her waiting. Here's a letter, Mother.

150

MRS. CRILLY (*looking at letter*) : When did it come, Anna.
ANNA : It's just handed in. (ANNA *goes out.* MRS. CRILLY *opens letter.*)
MRS. CRILLY : It's from the bank. They want me over there. What does the Bank Manager want with me, I wonder?
CRILLY : I've something to tell you, Marianne. I'll tell you in a while. (*He takes a turn up and down.*)
MRS. CRILLY : What do you want to tell me?
CRILLY : Prepare your mind, Marianne.
MRS. CRILLY : What is it?
CRILLY : I owe you money, Marianne.
MRS. CRILLY : Money! How do you owe me money?
CRILLY : That cute boy, James Covey, who took in all the town . . .
MRS. CRILLY : Covey! My God! You backed a bill for him?
CRILLY : I'll make a clean breast of it, Marianne. I did.
MRS. CRILLY (*with fear in her voice*) : How much is it?
CRILLY (*walking away to window*) : I'll come to that, Marianne.
MRS. CRILLY : Did anyone back the bill with you?
CRILLY : I obliged the fellow. No one backed the bill with me.
MRS. CRILLY : Does anyone know of it?
CRILLY : No, Marianne.
MRS. CRILLY : The bank . . . Tell me what happened?
CRILLY : He wants to tell you.
MRS. CRILLY : We had five hundred pounds in the bank.
CRILLY : We had, Marianne.
MRS. CRILLY : Tell me how much was the bill?
CRILLY : There's no use beating about the bush. The bill was for four hundred pounds.
MRS. CRILLY : You've ruined us at last, Crofton Crilly.
CRILLY : You should never forgive me, Marianne. I'll go to America and begin life again.

151

MRS. CRILLY : And you expect me to find the money to pay your passage?

CRILLY : Something might develop.

MRS. CRILLY : We have no money left.

CRILLY : A hundred pounds, Marianne.

MRS. CRILLY : That's Anna's money.

CRILLY : Scollard should be satisfied.

MRS. CRILLY : Anna insists on getting her money.

CRILLY : She's like the rest of them, that girl! All for herself! But what you all see in that Scollard . . .

> (JAMES SCOLLARD *comes in.* ANNA *is behind him.* SCOLLARD *has an account book in his hand.*)

SCOLLARD : Good morning, Mrs. Crilly. Good morning, Mister Crilly.

MRS. CRILLY : Good morning, Mister Scollard.

> (CROFTON CRILLY *turns to go*).

ANNA : Don't go, Father.

SCOLLARD : Don't go, Mister Crilly. I have something particular to say to yourself and Mrs. Crilly.

MRS. CRILLY : Sit down, Mister Scollard.

> (ANNA *brings chairs and* SCOLLARD *sits centre.* ANNA *stands behind him.* MRS. CRILLY *sits left of him.*)

SCOLLARD : I have come to propose for the hand of your daughter, Miss Anna Crilly.

MRS. CRILLY : We have nothing to say against your proposal, Mister Scollard.

CRILLY : Won't you take something, James?

SCOLLARD : No, thanks, Mister Crilly. I never touch intoxicants.

> (CROFTON CRILLY *goes into shop.*)

MRS. CRILLY : We couldn't wish for a better match for Anna. But I feel bound to tell you, Mister Scollard, that we have had a very severe loss in our business.

ANNA : What is it, Mother?

152

MRS. CRILLY : Mister Crilly has made himself responsible
  for a bill on the bank.

SCOLLARD : In whose interest, Mrs. Crilly?

MRS. CRILLY : He backed a bill for James Covey. A bill for
  four hundred pounds.

ANNA : Oh, Mother!

MRS. CRILLY : It's a dead sure loss. I don't know what we
  are to do, Anna.

SCOLLARD : This is very bad, Mrs. Crilly.

  (CROFTON CRILLY comes back from shop. He brings in
    a glass of whiskey. He puts whiskey on chimney piece.)

MRS. CRILLY : The bank has taken over four hundred
  pounds from our account.

CRILLY : Perhaps Scollard . . .

SCOLLARD : What were you saying, Mister Crilly?

CRILLY : Oh, I was just thinking . . . about a bill, you
  know . . . If someone would go security for us in
  the bank . . .

ANNA : Father, what are you saying?

MRS. CRILLY : It is unnecessary to talk like that. In spite of
  your foolishness, we still have a balance at the bank.

ANNA : My portion comes from my grandmother.

SCOLLARD : May I ask, Mrs. Crilly, is Miss Crilly's portion
  safe?

MRS. CRILLY : It is safe, Mister Scollard.

SCOLLARD : I have been definitely appointed Master of the
  Workhouse, and I may say that Anna and myself
  are anxious to marry.

MRS. CRILLY : It needn't be soon, Mister Scollard.

SCOLLARD : After Easter, Mrs. Crilly.

MRS. CRILLY : But that's very soon.

SCOLLARD : I am anxious to settle down, Mrs. Crilly. I am
  on my way to a meeting of the Board of Guardians,
  but before I go I'd like to have some more information
  about your loss.

153

MRS. CRILLY : Anna's portion is not touched, but we could hardly afford to let the money go from us now.

SCOLLARD : Is that so, Mrs. Crilly?

MRS. CRILLY : Four hundred pounds is a very severe loss.

SCOLLARD : Very severe, indeed. Still, you understand, Mrs. Crilly, the difficulty of taking such a step as marriage without adequate provision.

CRILLY : Damn it all, man, Marianne and myself married without any provision at all.

MRS. CRILLY (bitterly) : Anna won't be such a fool as her mother.

CRILLY : Well, Scollard has his position, and we helped him to get it.

SCOLLARD : I acknowledge that.

ANNA : Isn't my portion a hundred pounds, Mother?

MRS. CRILLY : Yes, Anna. But I'd like to tell Mister Scollard that it would come as a strain on us to let the money go at once.

ANNA : But, Mother, wouldn't the money be safer with us?

MRS. CRILLY : Well, I'll leave the whole thing in the hands of Mister Scollard.

SCOLLARD (formally) : Anna and myself have been talking things over, Mrs. Crilly.

ANNA : And we don't want to begin life in a scrambling sort of way.

MRS. CRILLY : You won't want the whole of the money. I'll give you fifty pounds now.

CRILLY : And fifty when the first child is born.

ANNA : I won't be bargained over in that way.

SCOLLARD : I need only say this. Anna and myself were talking over affairs, and we came to the conclusion it would be best not to start with less than her full portion. (He rises.) I have to go to the Board Room now, for there is a meeting of the Guardians. (He goes towards the door.)

154

CRILLY : Won't you take a glass?

SCOLLARD : No, thanks, Mister Crilly. I never touch stimulants. Good day to you all.

(*He goes out.* CROFTON CRILLY *goes after him.*)

MRS. CRILLY : Anna, you won't be deprived of your money.

ANNA : Then what is the difficulty, Mother?

MRS. CRILLY : Let half the money remain with us for a while.

ANNA : But, Mother, if I don't get all my money, what security have I that what's left will be good in six months or a year?

MRS. CRILLY : I'll watch the money for you, Anna.

ANNA : It's hard to keep hold on money in a town where business is going down.

MRS. CRILLY : Fifty pounds will be given you and fifty pounds will be kept safe for you.

ANNA : Fifty pounds! There is not a small farmer comes into the shop but his daughter has more of a dowry than fifty pounds.

MRS. CRILLY : You know the way we are situated. If you insist on getting a hundred pounds, we'll have to make an overdraft on the bank and, in the way business is, I don't know how we'll ever recover it.

ANNA : There won't be much left of a hundred when we get what suits us in furniture.

MRS. CRILLY : I could let you have some furniture.

ANNA : No, Mother. We want to start in a way that will have no reminders of this house.

MRS. CRILLY : You want all your money down?

ANNA : All of it, Mother.

MRS. CRILLY : You'll have to get it so. But you're very hard, Anna.

ANNA : This house would teach anyone to look after themselves.

155

MRS. CRILLY : Come upstairs. (CROFTON CRILLY *comes in from shop.* ANNA *goes* L.) Four hundred pounds of a loss. A hundred pounds with that. I'm terrified when I think. (*She goes after* ANNA.)

(CROFTON CRILLY *comes in from shop.*)

CRILLY : I don't know what Marianne is to do at all. She has a shocking lot to contend with. Can anything be got from the old man, I wonder?

(ALBERT CRILLY *comes in from door* L.)

CRILLY : What's the news in town, Albert?
ALBERT : They say you backed a bill for Covey.
CRILLY : If your mother hears that kind of talk she'll be vexed, Albert.
ALBERT : But did you back the bill?
CRILLY : For Heaven's sake, let me alone. Yes, I backed the bill.
ALBERT : How much?
CRILLY : You'll hear all about it from your mother.
ALBERT : They say it was for four hundred.
CRILLY : The worst of this town is that it has nothing to do except talk about other people's affairs.
ALBERT : 'Pon my word, Father, the mother will have to take out a mandamus against you.
CRILLY : Don't talk to me in that way, Albert.
ALBERT : It's scandalous, really. I expect you've ruined the business.
CRILLY : I hate the world and all that goes on in it.
ALBERT : I believe you've done for the business. Me, I'm leaving.
CRILLY : So you've got the job, Albert.
ALBERT : Temporary clerkship in the Land Department.
CRILLY : Ah, Albert, I wish I were getting your chance. You've something to do before you go, remember.

ALBERT : The stores inspection? There's enough in it for me for a new suit of clothes. With the money down I could get two suits, making payments for the second one afterwards.

CRILLY : Now don't let us down about that inspection job, Albert!

ALBERT : Corrupt practices are being invoked in passing!

CRILLY : Now let me tell you something, Albert. The old man is inclined to forget there was a deficiency there. Don't clap hands behind the bird!

ALBERT : You mean I'm to pass over the deficiency in the stores?

CRILLY : If you do, nothing will be known. The old man won't have to fork out his money to any Board of Guardians. And, believe me, the less money that's taken out of this house, the better for all concerned.

ALBERT : How am I to know there won't be three or four with me when I'm taking the inspection?

CRILLY : Well, Albert, all I say to you is—don't clap hands behind the bird.

(THOMAS MUSKERRY *comes in from livingroom. He looks looser, shabbier than when in the office of the Workhouse. As he enters,* CROFTON CRILLY *and* ALBERT *go into shop.* MUSKERRY *goes to the cupboard and opens it.*)

MRS CRILLY (*behind him*) : What has happened?

MUSKERRY : The good meat that I brought in! Pulled out of the basket! The cat has mangled it.

MRS. CRILLY : It was not the place to put meat. (*As he looks at her reprovingly.*) O, I know I shouldn't speak to you like that!

MUSKERRY : Not like to one of your children, Marianne.

MRS. CRILLY (*conciliatory*) : I'll see that it will be put in its proper place. You should let Anna . . .

MUSKERRY : I'm disappointed in Anna Crilly. A share in this shop was to go to her, but I'll hoard it with my own money.

MRS. CRILLY (*something of a plea in her voice*) : Don't be condemning of what goes on in the house at present. Anna, maybe, has been forgetful about bringing your soup to you.

MUSKERRY : That and other things.

MRS. CRILLY : I needn't say anything now on her behalf. Anna is getting married and taking her money away from us.

MUSKERRY : Anna getting married. This was kept from me. And who is Anna getting married to?

MRS. CRILLY : To James Scollard.

MUSKERRY : To James Scollard! And so Anna is getting married to my successor, James Scollard! My successor! How well I knew there was some such scheme in shifting me out of my mastership! And Anna Crilly was against me all the time. Well, well, well! I'll remember this.

MRS. CRILLY : Now don't remember us only for what is upsetting in us. You're here, and we want to make our own of you.

MUSKERRY : I have been made think that everyone under this roof has their place but me.

MRS. CRILLY : Stay here. Your soup will be ready by now, and I'll bring it to you myself.

(*She goes back into the livingroom.* MUSKERRY *places himself on the horse-hair sofa. In a while* MRS. CRILLY *returns with a bowl of soup which she places on a low table before him, then goes back.* MUSKERRY *takes his soup. As he does, in the distance is heard the playing of bagpipes. The sound is heard, lost, and heard again.* MUSKERRY *listens.* CHRISTY CLARKE *enters from the shop.*)

158

CHRISTY : Mister Muskerry.

MUSKERRY : Oh, it's you, Christy Clarke.

CHRISTY : I have brought more than myself.

MUSKERRY : But no one better, Christy.

CHRISTY : Wait till you see who I've brought. A particular old friend of yours, Mister Muskerry.

> (Behind CHRISTY comes a man of MUSKERRY'S age, but holding himself very upright. He wears glasses and carries a walking stick.)

THE MAN (advancing) : Thomas! Thomas Muskerry!

MUSKERRY (rising) : It can't be . . . Peter Macnabo?

MACNABO : Peter Macnabo come into your vicinity at last, Thomas.

MUSKERRY : Peter Macnabo that I used to course hares with!

MACNABO : We were spry fellows in the years back, Thomas.

MUSKERRY : And you're out of your mastership, Peter?

MACNABO : Out of it and well out of it.

MUSKERRY : And I'm out of my Garrisowen position. (Rather pitifully.) Did you hear that, Peter?

MACNABO : We're both unspancelled, Thomas. (He puts his stick down. CHRISTY CLARKE takes his hat and finds a a place to put it. The two old men stand looking at each other.)

MUSKERRY : Ah, Peter, if you had come to me where I was! The place I could have showed you! It was as fitted for me as the nest for the wren! This isn't my place, Peter. I'm here temporarily, living with family. And what way are you?

MACNABO : I'm at large. That's all I'll say about myself at present. I'm at large.

MUSKERRY : Well, you're in Garrisowen. You're in my domain. Peter, sit down! Christy Clarke, go into the shop and bring me out the best bottle of Mountain

Dew that they have. And glasses, Christy! Well, well, Peter. Peter Macnabo, it makes me feel hearty again to see you.

MACNABO : You say my name as you used to say it. Do you remember what the name means?

MUSKERRY : I disremember.

MACNABO : Mac na Boohie. Son of Victory.

MUSKERRY : These old names. I have one myself. We're of the old stock, Peter.

MACNABO : Macnabo and Muskerry!

MUSKERRY (*smiling*) : It sounds like an establishment, Peter.
    (CHRISTY CLARKE *brings in bottle and glasses.*)

MUSKERRY : You'll have dinner with me here. (*He looks around, but without much assurance.*) I'll see to it that it is in style. I've a grand-daughter, and if she puts her mind on something her grandfather wants, she can make a good gooseberry tart.

MACNABO : No, Thomas. The fact is, I'm on my rounds.

MUSKERRY : Your rounds, man?

MACNABO : Yes, Thomas. Besides coming to Garrisowen for the gratifying purpose of seeing an old friend, I'm here on business. I'm going further. But I'll be back again. I expect to make Garrisowen my headquarters.

MUSKERRY (*filling the glasses and handing him one*) : You'd be very welcome here, Peter.

MACNABO : The best thing that anybody ever did for me was to get me out of that place.

MUSKERRY : Out of the mastership of the Workhouse?

MACNABO : Out of the mastership of the Workhouse. And you're well out of it, too, Thomas.

MUSKERRY : It wasn't of my own will and wish—I'll have to say that, Peter.

MACNABO : They started proceedings against me—an inquiry they called it—by their Jacks-in-office. At first I was downed in myself—I thought my life was

160

ruined. Then, one morning I woke up and said to myself—You're getting out of a workhouse, you're getting away from pauperism, from Boards of Guardians squabbling over this and that. Take what they give you for your service, and go.

MUSKERRY : Had you a place to go to, Peter?

MACNABO : I'm finding it. A place where people are making things.

MUSKERRY : Making things?

MACNABO : Behind the walls of a workhouse—workhouse indeed! we're apt to forget that people live by making things.

(PETER MACNABO *takes three objects from his pocket and places them on table.*)

MUSKERRY : Pipes! Clay pipes!

MACNABO : Pipes of Irish clay—pipes that every man used to smoke in our day. They're gone out of fashion, and men will only smoke pipes that are manufactured for them across the sea. Where do you see people smoking pipes of Irish clay now, Thomas?

MUSKERRY : They smoke them at wakes.

MACNABO : You've said it. Before we bury our dead we smoke pipes of Irish clay. That's what we do with pipes we could be selling by the thousands and have hundreds of men on their benches working on them. And doesn't that tell you something of the state of affairs we've got into? Workhouse miscalled! Towns where nothing is made and people only think of jobs and pensions! And what is before us, I ask you? Bankruptcy! Bankruptcy in all directions!

MUSKERRY : You're a surprising man, Peter.

MACNABO : I surprise you, do I? I surprised myself when it all came over me. Look at this town! What do you see?

161

MUSKERRY : I want no part in it at all!

MACNABO : Why don't you want to have part in it? Because there's nothing to have part in except bankruptcy—bankruptcy.

MUSKERRY : Around what age are you, Peter?

MACNABO : Around the same age as yourself, Thomas.

MUSKERRY : You talk like a man who has the world before him.

MACNABO : And so I have. For ten years, anyway.

CHRISTY : I hope that Mr. Macnabo will talk to everybody in the town.

MUSKERRY : He has won your suffrage, Christy.

CHRISTY : And he's going to give me work.

MUSKERRY : You're no longer the Workhouse Master, Peter?

MACNABO : Nor are you, Thomas.

MUSKERRY : I was made into one. I think in my heart I'll be one for the rest of my days. I'll give you a good dinner here, Peter, and you'll tell me what mission you're on.

MACNABO : Well, it's not to preach, though here I'm indulging in that. There are my pipes of clay. I'm in Garrisowen because they're made here.

MUSKERRY : And how did you find that out? I only came on it myself by accident. Two old men in a shop make them. But what can they gain out of them at a penny a pipe?

MACNABO : They don't know how to sell them. The first thing I'll set up is a stall in the market for them. They never thought of doing that, but they'll sell pipes of clay by the dozen when they do. And as for their little shop, I'll take it over and enlarge it, putting into it the money I've got. I'll sell the pipes through Ireland when I've a dozen hands working for me. Garrisowen Macnabo Pipe—the pipe of Irish clay.

162

I'll have them sold in the capital. I'll have them sold across the sea. And here's the boy who's going to be my righthand man.

CHRISTY : I will indeed.

MACNABO : A new appearance will be on the town.

MUSKERRY : Maybe you'll be able to do it, Peter.

MACNABO : In a while I'll take out ten of your workhouse lads and have them making clay pipes, not for wakes, but for the men of Ireland who enjoy puffing tobacco. And I've found a poem that I'll have wrapped round every pipe, and that men will say to themselves as they pull on it, and that will spread the fame of the Macnabo pipe of clay all over the country. Not forgetting to remind them that Macnabo means Son of Victory.

(*He reads*) :

All the old haunts, and the dear friends, all the things
    I used to do,
The hopes and dreams of boyhood days, they all pass
    me in view;
And I'm thinking I am there again and beside sweet
    Dublin Bay,
I'm strolling on the Liffey banks or I'm bathing down
    at Bray,
I'm basking in the Phoenix Park, while the birds sing
    merrily.
The fresh winds waft the atmosphere of the moun-
    tains and the sea,
Or perhaps I'm on the Lucan Road, eating berries
    large and ripe,
When I send the smoke a-curling from my soft clay
    Irish pipe.*

* The Gael, New York, Sept., 1904.

MACNABO : I don't know what directed me to that poem, but it was a find, if ever there was one. There will be Irishmen all over the United States of America saying that poem to themselves as they pull on the pipe of clay from far-off Garrisowen.

MUSKERRY : You've wonderful notions, Peter. I did not know it was in you to have—I may call them— sweeping ideas.

MACNABO : I didn't know it myself until they discharged me from Dooard Workhouse. God help me! I thought I was Master there, but I was just as much of a pauper as any old fellow in the wards.

MUSKERRY : Let you never say that, Peter. It was a great thing to exercise the authority of a Master of a Workhouse, giving one's mind to the poor and homeless. We'll have a talk about it at our dinner here.

MACNABO : Macnabo and Muskerry.

MUSKERRY : Peter! Peter! Did you see these names over an establishment?

MACNABO : It's not that I saw them, but that I will see them. Macnabo and Muskerry, Manufacturers of the Garrisowen Pipes of Clay.

MUSKERRY : Ah, Peter, your enthusiasm carries you beyond the bounds. If I were forty years younger!

MACNABO : You're young enough, Thomas. Isn't he, Christy Clarke?

CHRISTY (*earnestly*) : Mister Muskerry is a man of great capacity.

MUSKERRY : What you want, if I understand aright, Peter, is a partner and he'd have to be a man with money.

MACNABO : The same amount of money which I have, Thomas, which is the same amount as you have.

MUSKERRY : I'll talk to you after a while, Peter, when your mind is composed.

MACNABO : The minute I heard I could acquire the little business of Garrisowen, I said to myself, " Thomas Muskerry must go with me in this." But I'm not offering a partnership at present. I'm going to Mohill where there's another shop, and when I come back we'll have our agreements. I'll find you here, Thomas?

MUSKERRY : I won't be here. Will I, Christy?

CHRISTY : I don't know, Mister Muskerry.

MUSKERRY : Your mother would come and look after me if I were living in more rural surroundings.

CHRISTY : She would indeed, Mister Muskerry.

MUSKERRY : You'll not be going off now, Peter. We'll have dinner here. I'll see that it will be as good as you'll get between here and Mohill.

MACNABO : No, Thomas. I'm taking the train almost immediately.

MUSKERRY : I take it bad of you that you won't spend a day with me in memory of old times.

MACNABO : Very pleasant times they were, too, Thomas, and very agreeable to look back on. I'll say good-bye to you now, and I'm glad to see you looking . . .

MUSKERRY : I'm not looking as grand as you are, Peter.

MACNABO : I was low down until this calling of mine gave me a lift up. It will do the same for you, Thomas— an uplift.

MUSKERRY : Go on another train. Stay here and let me provide for you.

MACNABO : The Master is in the very words you speak, Thomas. You liked the Mastership! So did I! But there's better than that! It is to give a hand where something is being made. And that's what we'll do, Thomas. And in this town, too.

(*They grasp hands.*)

165

MUSKERRY : Well, whatever comes or goes, we'll meet some place, and it uplifts me to know that such a hearty man is in the world.

MACNABO : Macnabo and Muskerry!

(*He goes off.*)

CHRISTY : Isn't it well for me that he picked me to help him?

MUSKERRY : It is, Christy, it is. (*He seats himself in the armchair.*) And here are the pipes of clay that he is making so much of! (*He takes up a pipe.*) No doubt he'll do something and it will be to your benefit, Christy. But I find it hard to depart from the notion I had of quiet days by myself in rural surroundings. But if anybody could make me alter that notion it would be Peter Macnabo. And now I'll try that pipe of his. It's a long time since a pipe of Irish clay was in my mouth.

(*He settles down, puts tobacco in one of the clay pipes on the table, lights it and begins to smoke.*)

MUSKERRY : What was that poem that pleased him so much. Read it to me, Christy.

(ALBERT *comes in from shop.*)

ALBERT : Good morning, Grandpapa! I brought your newspaper.

MUSKERRY : I'm glad to have your attention, sir.

ALBERT : You'll be more glad to hear that I've been made inspector of the stores.

MUSKERRY : And why would I be glad of that?

ALBERT : We'll see you through, you know.

MUSKERRY : I know nothing at all of what's in your mind, and you're a damn infernal puppy.

ALBERT : Somebody you know is in the shop—Felix Tournour.

MUSKERRY : Felix Tournour? Who gave him leave to be in the town at this hour of the day?

166

ALBERT : Well, the way things are now, I suppose he gave himself leave.

MUSKERRY : Rank insubordination! That's what it will all come to!

ALBERT : Well, maybe the reins aren't held as tight as they used to be, Grandpapa!

MUSKERRY : Send Tournour in to me.

ALBERT (*talking into shop*) : You're wanted here, Tournour. Come in now, or I'll entertain the Master with " The Devil's Rambles."

(FELIX TOURNOUR *enters. He looks prosperous. He has a loud check suit and wears a red tie and peaked cap.*)

ALBERT : The Master wants to speak to you, Tournour.

TOURNOUR : What Master?

ALBERT : The boss, Tournour, the boss.

MUSKERRY : I want you, and that's enough for you, Tournour.

ALBERT : I suppose you don't know, Grandpapa, that Tournour has a middling high position in the Workhouse now.

MUSKERRY : What are you saying?

ALBERT : Tournour is the Ward Master now.

MUSKERRY : I wasn't given any notice of that.

ALBERT : Eh, Tournour——

" The Devil went out for a ramble at night
Through Garrisowen Workhouse to see every sight,
He saw Felix Tournour . . ."

(*With great boldness* TOURNOUR *takes a position with his back to the fire. He seems to take possession of the room.*)

TOURNOUR : " He saw one in comfort, of that you'll be sure,
With his back to the fire stands Felix Tournour."

ALBERT : Well, so-long, gents. (*He goes out by the shop door.*)

MUSKERRY : Let me see you, Tournour.

TOURNOUR : I'm plain to be seen.

MUSKERRY : Who recommended you for Ward Master?

TOURNOUR : Them that had the power.

MUSKERRY : I would not have done it, Tournour.

TOURNOUR : No. And still d'ye see, I'm up and not down. Well, I'll be going.

MUSKERRY : Come back here, Tournour. I made it a rule that no Ward Master should let drink be brought in to the paupers.

TOURNOUR : It's a pity you're not Master still!

MUSKERRY : What are you saying?

TOURNOUR : It's a pity you're not still the Master over us.

MUSKERRY : Tournour, you're forgetting yourself.

TOURNOUR : Well, maybe, you are still the Master.

MUSKERRY : How dare you speak to me with such effrontery? How dare you?

TOURNOUR : I dunno. I'm going away now, if your honour has nothing more to say to me. (*He turns to go out.*)

MUSKERRY : You shall not. You shall not, I say.

TOURNOUR : What?

MUSKERRY : You shall not go away until you've apologised to me.

TOURNOUR : Don't be talking, Thomas Muskerry. You're not Master over me.

MUSKERRY : Not Master over you!

TOURNOUR : No. There's an end to your sway, Mister Muskerry.

MUSKERRY : Go out of the house! No, stay there. You think I'm out of the Workhouse. No. That's not so. I've claims, great claims, on it still. Not for nothing was I there for over thirty years, the pattern for the officials of Ireland.

TOURNOUR : Twenty-nine years, I'm telling you.

MUSKERRY : The Guardians will take account of me.

TOURNOUR : And maybe they would, too.

MUSKERRY : What's that you're saying?

TOURNOUR : The Guardians might take account of Thomas
Muskerry in a way he mightn't like. (*He goes towards
the door.*)

MUSKERRY : Come back here, Felix Tournour.

TOURNOUR : I'm not a sub-servant to you.

MUSKERRY : Stand before me.

TOURNOUR : You and you're before me! Your back to
heaven and your belly to hell!

MUSKERRY : Go away. Go away out of this.

TOURNOUR : Don't try to down-face me. I know something about you.

MUSKERRY : About me!

TOURNOUR : Aye, you and your hundred tons of coal.
(MUSKERRY *goes back from him.*) Great claims on the
Workhouse, have you? The Guardians will take
account of you. Will they? Talk to them about the
hundred tons of coal. Go and do that, my pattern for
the officials of Ireland!

(TOURNOUR *goes out by the shop.* MUSKERRY *stands
with his hands on the arm-chair.*)

MUSKERRY : This minute I'll go down to the Guardians
and make my complaint. My coat needs brushing.
(*He takes off his coat and brushing it goes to the window.*)
I'm letting myself get shabby in this place. I'm
losing my uprightness. I'll do more than brush my
coat. I'll go down to the Guardians and pay them
back their fifty pounds.

(*In great agitation* MUSKERRY *attends to his appearance. Standing before a small mirror, with a scissors
he has taken up, he trims his beard.* ANNA CRILLY
*comes in from shop, measures a piece of furniture
with tape and moves on as if calculating.* ALBERT CRILLY,
a book of tailor's patterns in his hand, comes after her.)

ALBERT : Hey, Anna! What's your opinion of this heather-colour stuff?

(*One following the other, they go into the living-rooms.*)

MUSKERRY : I'm shocked at the state I've let myself get into!

(MRS. CRILLY *comes from livingrooms, account books in her hand.*)

MRS. CRILLY (*noticing his agitation*) : What has come over you?

MUSKERRY : A certain person has spoken to me in a way I'll never submit to be spoken to again.

MRS. CRILLY : If it's no more than speaking to you . . .

MUSKERRY : Felix Tournour knows about the coal, Marianne. He can disgrace me before the world.

MRS. CRILLY : The Master can deal with him.

MUSKERRY : The Master?

MRS. CRILLY : I mean Mister Scollard.

MUSKERRY : I'll have nothing to do with him! I'm going before the Board of Guardians and I'll pay them back their fifty pounds.

MRS. CRILLY : Fifty pounds! From what place is fifty pounds to come so easily?

MUSKERRY : I'll ask you to give me the fifty pounds, Marianne.

MRS. CRILLY : I'll do no such thing.

MUSKERRY : There is my money in the shop.

MRS. CRILLY : I'm at great losses since you came here.

MUSKERRY : I'm at greater losses, Marianne.

MRS. CRILLY : What losses are you at?

MUSKERRY : The loss of my trust, the loss of my dignity, my self-respect, and . . .

MRS. CRILLY : Oh, what can I say to you when you talk like that? But I think we did all we could for you.

170

MUSKERRY : I'm going out to pay back the Guardians the
    sum due to them from me. I want fifty pounds from
    you. I claim it, and I've a right to claim it.

MRS. CRILLY : We have no money at all. Listen! Crofton
    Crilly backed a bill from James Covey, and the bank
    has taken over what we had in our account—four
    hundred pounds.

MUSKERRY (*as if hearing something incredible*) : Four hundred
    pounds!

MRS. CRILLY : Yes. Four hundred pounds.

MUSKERRY (*with strong moral feeling*) : He backed a bill for
    four hundred pounds! And do you think, Marianne
    Crilly, there can be luck or grace in a house where
    such a thing could happen? There could be no good
    prayers in a house like this. I'll go out of this house
    and I'll never put foot into it again.

    (*He takes up hat and stick.*)

MRS. CRILLY : And where will you go?

MUSKERRY : I'll go before the Board of Guardians and I'll
    ask them to provide for me.

MRS. CRILLY : What do you want me to do?

MUSKERRY : Give me fifty pounds so that I can pay them
    off now.

MRS. CRILLY (*desperately*) : Haven't I told you?

MUSKERRY : You must have in the bank what would save
    my name.

MRS. CRILLY : In the bank, nothing. Nothing at all!

MUSKERRY (*holding out his hands to her*) : Draw on all that
    you own to give me this money!

MRS. CRILLY : Don't be unreasonable. I have to provide
    for my children.

MUSKERRY : Your children. Yes, you have to provide for
    them. I provided for them long enough. And now
    you would take my place, my honour, and my self-
    respect, and provide for them over again.

171

      (He goes to the door.)

I thought it was for ever, mastership. I thought that nothing could humble me. I have been humbled. I tell you this, Marianne. The meanest person in the pauper's ward has more consideration than I have in this house.

MRS. CRILLY : Come back.

MUSKERRY : I go where I have to go.

      (He goes out through shop. ANNA *enters from living-rooms.)*

MRS. CRILLY *(quite spent)* : He has gone down to the Work-house. He says he will ask the Guardians to provide for him.

ANNA : Mister Scollard will see that he doesn't put us in a bad position before the town.

MRS. CRILLY : I suppose so. Here is your cheque, Anna.

ANNA : I'm thankful, Mother.

MRS. CRILLY : It's the last cheque I'll be able to make out. The bank . . . Oh, the Bank . . . *(She puts her hand to her head as she goes into shop.* ANNA CRILLY *resumes measuring pieces of furniture.)*

CURTAIN

172

ACT FOUR

The Infirm Ward in the Workhouse. Entrance from Corridor right. Forward, left, are three beds with bedding folded upon them. Back left is door leading into select ward. The door is closed, and a large key is in lock, fireplace with a grating round it is left. Back right is a window with little leaded panes.

It is noon on a May day, but the light inside the ward is feeble. Myles Gorman is seated on a bench, mending the bag of his pipes. Shanley is seated at the fire. Thomas Muskerry enters from the corridor. He wears his own clothes, but he has let them get into disorder. His hair and beard are disordered, and he seems very much broken down. Nevertheless, he looks as if his mind was composed.

MUSKERRY : It's dark here, Michael.

SHANLEY : It is, sir.

MUSKERRY : I find it very spiritless after coming up from the chapel. Don't pass your whole day here. Go down to the yard. (*He stands before the window.*) This is the first fine day, and you ought to go out along the country road. Ask the Master for leave. It is the month of May, and you'll be glad of the sight of the grass and the smell of the bushes.

GORMAN : You'll hear my pipes upon the road to-day.

(*An old pauper comes into the ward. His face looks bleached. He has the handle of a sweeping-brush for a staff. He moves about the ward muttering to himself.*)

OLD PAUPER (*as if thinking aloud*) : I was at twelve o'clock Mass. Now one o'clock would be a late Mass. I was at Mass at one o'clock. Wouldn't that be a long time to keep a priest and he fasting the whole time?

173

MUSKERRY (*at window*) : Now here's a remarkable thing. I venture to think that the like of this has never happened before. Here are the bees swarming at the window-pane.

SHANLEY : Myles Gorman will be glad to hear that buzzing.

GORMAN : The buzzing at the pane would let me know that the air is nice for a journey. You'll hear my pipes on the road, and that's as sure as the right hand is on my body.

SHANLEY (*to* MUSKERRY) : I was telling this old fellow what brought you into the Workhouse. Living in a bad house—living with your own. And that's what brought him into the Workhouse. And that's what brought me here, too.

(*He goes out.*)

MUSKERRY : I went before a meeting of the Guardians and I told them I owed them the whole of my year's pension. Then I got some sort of a stroke and broke down, and the Guardians gave me the Select Ward in there for myself.

SHANLEY : It's right that you should have the little room and not have to make down the pauper's bed with the rest of us.

MUSKERRY : Well, to-day I'm leaving this place.

SHANLEY : And where are you going? Mister Muskerry?

MUSKERRY : I'm going to a place of my own. (*He goes into the room.*)

OLD MAN WITH STAFF : Skibbereen! That's where the people died when there was the hunger. Men and women without coffins or even their clothes off. Just buried. Skibbereen I remember well for I was a whole man then. And the village. For there are people living in it yet. They didn't all die. (*He goes out.*)

SHANLEY : They'll have to have somebody else in the Select Ward this evening. That's what they were talking about. The nuns are sending a patient up here. I suppose the Ward Master will be here to regulate the room.

OLD MAN : Felix Tournour! That's the lad that will be coming in with his hand up like the gander after beating down a child!

(CHRISTY CLARKE enters. He carries a small portmanteau.)

CHRISTY : Is Mister Muskerry here?

OLD MAN : He's in the room. (A sound of water splashing and the movements of a heavy person are heard.) Will you be speaking with him, young fellow?

CHRISTY : I will.

OLD MAN : Well, tell him from me, Mickie Cripes, that I don't want to be in the way of Felix Tournour. Me and the rest of us are going to the yard, but we'll see Mister Muskerry when he's going away. (He goes out.)

MUSKERRY (within) : Is that you, Christy Clarke?

CHRISTY : It is, Mister Muskerry.

MUSKERRY : Have you any news, Christy?

CHRISTY : Well, my mother is in the cottage and she's expecting you to-day.

MUSKERRY : I'll be in the cottage to-day, Christy. I'm cleaning myself. (A sound of splashing and moving about.) The Guardians were good to get the little house for me. I'd as leave be there as in a mansion. There's about half an acre of land to the place, and I'll do work on the ground from time to time, for it's a good thing for a man to get the smell of the clay.

CHRISTY : And how are you in health, Mister Muskerry?

MUSKERRY : I'm very well in health. I was anointed, you know, and after that I mended miraculously.

175

CHRISTY : And I've been told that the business of your pension is settled.

MUSKERRY : They asked me to realize my pension, and I did, and I've got a good sum of money. (*He comes out of room. He has on trousers, coat and starched shirt. The shirt seems crushed.*) On Saturdays I'll do my marketing. I'll come into town and buy my provisions for Sunday and the days after.

CHRISTY : It will be good for us to see you.

MUSKERRY (*sitting down on a chair*) : I was dreaming of new things all last night. New shirts, new sheets, everything new.

CHRISTY : Mister Macnabo can't get it in his mind that you're leaving the town behind you.

MUSKERRY : My old friend Peter! Is he back in the town, Christy?

CHRISTY : He and I have been readying the work benches and whitewashing the walls of the clay pipe establishment.

MUSKERRY : Establishment! That's a very firm word, Christy.

CHRISTY : It is. Macnabo and Muskerry would look well over it, he says.

MUSKERRY : Since I've been here, Christy, I've come to know something about myself.

CHRISTY : And what is that, Mister Muskerry?

MUSKERRY : That I'm an old man, Christy. And what does an old man do? He looks on and he looks back. Peter Macnabo is the same age as myself, but he's not an old man. I couldn't be with him.

CHRISTY (*disappointed*) : Could you not, Mister Muskerry?

MUSKERRY : I'll live in the cottage with your mother to help me, but I won't be so much of a hermit, Christy, that I won't know how you and your patron are making out with your pipes of Irish clay.

176

CHRISTY : It's lucky for me that he's taking me in with him.

MUSKERRY : It is, Christy. And I wouldn't be surprised if it came to be a real success and that you'll have a career out of it, or out of something next to it.

CHRISTY : If it doesn't succeed . . . Do you know what Mr. Macnabo says?

MUSKERRY : My friend Peter has a powerful way of expressing himself.

CHRISTY : The town will be left to people who have bankruptcy inside and outside of themselves.

MUSKERRY (*impressed by the way* CHRISTY *delivers himself of the saying*) : You'll remember that, Christy.

CHRISTY : There's a lot of meaning in it, Mister Muskerry.

MUSKERRY : Well, you'll be here, Christy, and I'll be nearby, and I'll see you go along by leaps and bounds.

CHRISTY : And maybe I'll be able to be of some service to you. (*He brings the portmanteau to him.*) I got this for you. You could put your shirts into it.

MUSKERRY : Well, isn't that good of you, Christy. I thank you heartily for your thoughtfulness. Shirts, did you say.

CHRISTY : They were on my mind because I saw them drying before the fire in my mother's house, but I forgot to bring them.

MUSKERRY : I'd look better if I had a fresher shirt. I wish I could get one before I leave this place.

CHRISTY : Will I run off and get one for you?

MUSKERRY : Would you? Christy? Would it be too much trouble? (MUSKERRY *rises.*)

CHRISTY : I'll go now.

MUSKERRY : You're a very willing boy, Christy, and you're sure to get on. (*He goes to a little mirror on the wall.*) I'm white and loose of flesh, and that's not a good sign with me, Christy. I'll tell you something. If I were staying here to-night, it's the pauper's bed I'd have to sleep on.

(MRS. CRILLY *comes to the door.*)

MRS. CRILLY : Well, I see you're making ready for your departure.

MUSKERRY (*who has become uneasy*) : I am ready for my departure.

MRS. CRILLY : And this young man has come for you, I suppose?

MUSKERRY : This young man is minding his own business.

CHRISTY (*to* MRS. CRILLY) : I'm going out now to get a shirt for the Master.

MRS. CRILLY : A starched shirt, I suppose, Christy. Go down to our house and tell Mary to give you one of the shirts that are folded up.

MUSKERRY : The boy will go where he was bid go.

MRS. CRILLY : Oh, very well. Run, Christy and do the message for the Master.

(CHRISTY CLARKE *goes out.*)

MUSKERRY : I don't know what brought you here to-day.

MRS. CRILLY : Well, I wanted to see you.

MUSKERRY : I'd be glad to see you when I was settled down.

MRS. CRILLY : Settled in the cottage?

MUSKERRY : Yes, ma'am.

MRS. CRILLY (*in an outburst which she hadn't been able to restrain*) : No one of us will ever go near the place.

MUSKERRY : Well, you'll please yourself.

MRS. CRILLY : You put a slight on all of us when you go there to live.

MUSKERRY : I have lived with you to my loss.

MRS. CRILLY : Our house is the best house in town, and I'm the nearest person to you.

MUSKERRY : Say nothing more about that.

MRS. CRILLY : Well, maybe you do right to have your own residence. But you oughtn't to go there as if you were forsaking us altogether.

178

MUSKERRY : What you you mean by forsaking you altogether?

MRS. CRILLY : When you leave this place and do not even turn your step in our direction, it's a sign to all who want to know that you forsake us altogether.

MUSKERRY : What do you want me to do?

MRS. CRILLY : Come up to Cross Street with me, have dinner and spend the night with us. People will have less to talk about if you do that.

MUSKERRY : You always have a scheme.

MRS. CRILLY : Come with us for the evening itself.

MUSKERRY : I wish you wouldn't trouble me, woman. Can't you see that when I go out of this I want to go to my own place.

MRS. CRILLY : What odds does it make? You can go there to-morrow.

MUSKERRY : Preparations are made for me.

MRS. CRILLY : How do you know what preparations?

MUSKERRY : Two pounds of the best beef steak were ordered to be sent there to-day.

MRS. CRILLY : I wouldn't trust that woman, Mrs. Clarke, to cook potatoes.

MUSKERRY : Well, I trust her ma'am.

MRS. CRILLY (taking MUSKERRY's sleeve) : Don't go there to-day.

MUSKERRY : You're very anxious to get me to come with you. What do you want from me?

MRS. CRILLY : We want nothing from you—nothing that would be any loss to you to give us. But we're all depending on what business is left us. It is insecure. When it is known in the town that you have turned your back on us, everybody will close on us.

MUSKERRY : God knows that I did everything a man could for you and yours. I won't forget you. What days are left me, be they many or few, I want to live to myself.

MRS. CRILLY : Well do I know that—well do I know. (*She turns to him, her words heartfelt.*) Sure I lie awake at night, too tired to sleep, and long to get away from the things that are pressing in on me. I know that people are glad of their own way, and glad to live away from the people that are claiming things from them. When I heard the birds stirring I cried to be in some place where I won't hear the thing that's always knocking at my head. The business has to be minded. And it's slipping from us like water. And I can see foreclosure—bankruptcy.

(*With a gesture of profound distress* MUSKERRY *turns from her.*)

MRS. CRILLY : It's not like you to turn your back on us.

MUSKERRY : What more do you want me to do?

MRS. CRILLY : Stay with us for a while, so that we'll have the name of your support.

MUSKERRY : I'll come back in a week.

MRS. CRILLY : There's a reason for what I ask. The town must know you are with us from the time you leave this.

MUSKERRY : Will you never be done taking from me? I want to leave this and go to the place I have chosen for my own.

(MUSKERRY *puts his hand to his eyes. When he lowers his hand again* MRS. CRILLY *lays hers on it.* MUSKERRY *has been crying.*)

MRS. CRILLY : Only for the world is the way it is . . .

MUSKERRY : I thought the bees' humming was to send me on my way to something I wanted.

(CHRISTY CLARKE *comes in.* MRS. CRILLY *makes a sign to him begging him not to speak.*)

MUSKERRY : Well, Christy, I'll be sending you another message. (CHRISTY CLARKE, *very tense, stands still.*) Go to your mother and tell her . . .

CHRISTY : I met my mother outside.

MUSKERRY : Did she get the things that were sent to her?

CHRISTY : My mother was sent away from the cottage.

MUSKERRY : And who sent your mother away from the cottage?

CHRISTY (*like one who has suffered a great injury*) : Mrs. Crilly sent her away.

MUSKERRY : And why did you do that, ma'am?

MRS. CRILLY : I'm at fault. I sent Mary to help prepare the place for you, and the woman . . . she couldn't help it, I suppose . . . was impertinent to Mary.

MUSKERRY : Well, ma'am?

MRS. CRILLY (*drearily*) : I sent her away.

MUSKERRY : And so you take it on yourself to dispose of the servants in my house?

MRS. CRILLY : You'll take this woman's part against my daughter.

MUSKERRY : No, ma'am, I'll take no one's side, but I'll tell you this. I want my own life and I won't be interfered with.

MRS. CRILLY : I'm sorry for what occurred and in every way I can I'll make up for what I said and did.

MUSKERRY : I won't be interfered with, I tell you. From this day out I'm free of my own life. And now, Christy Clarke, go down stairs and tell the Master, Mister Scollard, that I want to see him.

(CHRISTY CLARKE *goes out*.)

MRS. CRILLY : I may as well tell you something else. None of the things you ordered were sent to the cottage.

MUSKERRY : Do you tell me that?

MRS. CRILLY : I went to the shop and everything you ordered was sent to our place.

MUSKERRY : And what is the meaning of that, ma'am?

MRS. CRILLY : If the town knew you were going away from us in a week we would have to put up our shutters.

181

MUSKERRY : Well, I'll walk out of this house, and when I come to the road I'll go my own way.

MRS. CRILLY : We can't prevent your doing that.

MUSKERRY : No, ma'am, you can't prevent that.

MRS. CRILLY : You have got your discharge . . .

MUSKERRY : I have given three hours' notice and I'll get my discharge now.

MRS. CRILLY (*at corridor door*) : We can't prevent you going if you have the doctor's discharge.

MUSKERRY : The doctor's discharge! He would have given it to me . . .

MRS. CRILLY : You can't leave without the doctor's sanction.

MUSKERRY : Out of this place I will go to-day.

> (JAMES SCOLLARD *enters.*)

SCOLLARD : I believe you want to see me, Mister Muskerry.

MUSKERRY : I do, Mister Scollard. I am leaving this house.

SCOLLARD : Such formalities as are necessary, Mister Muskerry . . .

MRS. CRILLY (*taking charge of the situation*) : First of all, has the doctor marked my father off the infirmary list?

SCOLLARD : No, Mrs. Crilly. Now that I recall the list, he has not.

MUSKERRY : I stayed a while in the chapel after Mass and I missed seeing him.

MRS. CRILLY : My father was seriously ill only a short time ago, and I do not believe he is in a fit state to leave the infirmary.

SCOLLARD : That certainly has to be considered. Without the doctor's sending you explicitly down to the body of the house you are hardly under my jurisdiction, Mister Muskerry.

MUSKERRY : I'll have to make a request of you then . . . request . . . Mister Scollard I ask you to give me leave to go out of the Workhouse for a day. You can do this on your own responsibility.

182

MRS. CRILLY : In his present state . . . it's not likely he would return to-night. Then, if anything happened to him your responsibility would be great.

MUSKERRY : I'm not one of the paupers . . . I'm . . . Thirty years the Master. I'll go out of this to-day without leave or licence from any of you.

SCOLLARD : As you know yourself, Mister Muskerry, it would be as much as my situation is worth to let you depart in that way.

MUSKERRY : Well, go I will.

SCOLLARD : I cannot permit it, Mister Muskerry. I say it with great respect.

MUSKERRY : How long will you keep me here?

SCOLLARD : Until the doctor visits the house.

MUSKERRY : That will be on Monday morning.

SCOLLARD : And this is Saturday, Mister Muskerry.

MUSKERRY : And where will you put me until Monday?

SCOLLARD : The old arrangements will continue. Can I do anything further for you, Mister Muskerry?

MUSKERRY : No, you can do nothing further for me. It's a great deal you have done for me! It's the pauper's bed you have given me! (*He goes into select ward.*)

(MRS. CRILLY *seats herself at table.* SCOLLARD *sits down.*)

MRS. CRILLY : The bank manager is in the town to-day, and there are people waiting to tell him whether my father goes to our house or goes away from us.

SCOLLARD : No doubt there are, Mrs. Crilly.

MRS. CRILLY : But you have nothing to do with that, Mister Scollard.

SCOLLARD : No, Mrs. Crilly.

MRS. CRILLY : I have my own battle to fight, and a hard battle it is. I have to make bits of myself to mind everything and be prepared for everything.

183

SCOLLARD : I understand your position, Mrs. Crilly, and I think I've leaned backwards a little to help you.

MRS. CRILLY : There are people who'd blame me, but they can't see into my mind.

SCOLLARD : Will you come down to the parlour, Mrs. Crilly?

MRS. CRILLY : Yes, I'll go down.

(She remains seated, looking out steadily before her. MYLES GORMAN comes in. He is dressed in his own clothes.)

SCOLLARD : Well, Gorman, what brings you back to the ward?

GORMAN : I just want to make some repair on my pipes, Master.

SCOLLARD : Very well, Gorman. You have your discharge and you are free to leave.

GORMAN : Oh, in a while I'll be taking the road.

SCOLLARD *(to MRS. CRILLY)* : These itinerants! I'm preparing a memorandum for the Local Government as to how to deal with them. Now, Mrs. Crilly, come down to the parlour.

MRS. CRILLY : Yes.

SCOLLARD : Anna is waiting to see you.

MRS. CRILLY *(rising)* : He will be well cared for here.

SCOLLARD : He will, Mrs. Crilly. I'll give him all my attention.

MRS. CRILLY : He expected to be in a different place to-day, but delay does little harm.

SCOLLARD : Come down to the parlour, Mrs. Crilly and drink a glass of wine with us.

MRS. CRILLY : He was threatened with something— apoplexy, it was. *(They go out.)*

(MYLES GORMAN *at the fire, is fixing the bag of his*
pipes. The door of the select ward opens and MUSKERRY
appears. He has had a stroke. His breathing makes a
noise in his mouth. As he moves he sags somewhat at
the right knee. He carries his right hand at his breast.
He moves slowly across ward. FELIX TOURNOUR
enters carrying a bunch of keys.)

TOURNOUR : And where are you going?

MUSKERRY (*in a thickened voice*) : Ow——out. (*Motioning*
with his left hand, he moves across ward, and goes out by
door of corridor.)

TOURNOUR : Well, you're not getting back to your
snuggery, my oul' cod. (*He goes into select ward and*
begins to pitch MUSKERRY'S *belongings into the outer*
ward. The pillows and covering of the bed are pitche
out.) And there's your holy picture and there's your
holy book. (*He throws them down. He comes ou*
with another book that is evidently a manuscript. He opens
it.) " Marianne born May 20th." The woman's
older than me. (*He turns pages and reads.*) " Thomas
Muskerry wrote this in his nineteenth year——

In the pleasant month of May,
When the lambkins sport and play,
As I roved out for recreation,
I spied a comely maid
Sequestered in the shade,
And on her beauty I gazed in admiration."

Well, the times are gone by when anybody would
make a jack-ass of himself by putting that down.
(*He reads*) :—

" I said, ' I greatly fear
That Mercury will draw near,
As once he appeared unto Venus,
Or as it might have been
To the Carthaginian Queen . . .' "

Had the man any sense at all when he was that ould?
Roving out on May mornings and watching lambkins
and comely maids. Did anybody ever do the like?
Felix Tournour is the boy who can better that.

> The Devil went out for a ramble at night,
> Through Garrisowen Workhouse to see every
>   sight,
> Deep dreaming that night of fast days before,
> Sagging the walls with the pull of his snore,
> In his chamber above Thomas Muskerry lay snug,
> When the Devil this summons roared in his lug—
> " Get up," said the Devil . . .

(MUSKERRY *comes back to the ward. He stands looking
stupidly at the heap* TOURNOUR *has thrown out.*
MUSKERRY *goes towards the open door of the select
ward.* FELIX TOURNOUR *closes the door deliberately,
turns the key and holds the key in his hand.*)

TOURNOUR : You've no more to do with your snug little
ward, Mister Muskerry. (*He puts the key in the bunch
and goes out.*)

MUSKERRY (*muttering with slack lips and cheeks*) : It's . . . It's
. . . the pau . . . pauper's bed they've given me.

GORMAN (*turning round his face*) : Who's there?

MUSKERRY : It's . . . It's Thomas Muskerry.

GORMAN : Is that the Master?

MUSKERRY : It's . . . It's the pauper's bed they've given me.

GORMAN : Can I give you a hand, Master?

MUSKERRY : I'll want to make . . . the bed. Give me a hand
to make the bed. Whose bed is this?

GORMAN : It's the middle bed, Master. It's my own bed.

MUSKERRY : What bed will I take then? (*helplessly.*)

GORMAN : My bed. I won't be here.

MUSKERRY : And where are you going?

GORMAN : I'm leaving the house this day. I'll be going
on the roads.

MUSKERRY : Myles . . . Myles Gorman. The man that was without family or relation. Myles Gorman. Help me to lay down the mattress. My own sheets and blankets are here. I needn't lie on a pauper's sheet. Where will you sleep to-night, Myles Gorman?

GORMAN : At Mrs. Molloy's, a house between this and the town of Ballinagh. I'll have the money to pay her by the time I get there. The oul' pipes will draw them, Master. I'll spread a sheet for you.

(They spread the sheet on the bed.)

MUSKERRY : Can you go down the stairs, Myles Gorman? I tried to get down the stairs, and my legs failed me.

GORMAN : One of the oul' men will lead me down.

MUSKERRY : Sure one of the men will lead me down, too.

(MYLES GORMAN spreads the cover on the bed. He stands up, lifts his pipes, and is ready to go out. MUSKERRY becomes more feeble. He puts himself on the bed.)

MUSKERRY : Myles . . . Myles Gorman . . . come back.

GORMAN : What will I do for you, Master?

MUSKERRY : Say a prayer for me.

GORMAN : What prayer will I say, Master?

MUSKERRY : Say " God be good to Thomas Muskerry."

GORMAN *(taking off his hat)* : God be good to Thomas Muskerry, the man who was good to the poor. Is that all, Master?

MUSKERRY : That's . . . that's all.

(GORMAN goes to the door.)

GORMAN : My pipes for the road!

(He goes out. There is a sound of heavy breathing from the bed. Then silence. The old pauper with the staff enters. He is crossing the ward when his attention is taken by the humming of the bees at the window pane. He listens for a moment.)

OLD PAUPER : A bright day, and the rain on their faces. That's what I saw. And we used to be coming from Mass and going to the coursing match. The hare flying and the dogs stretching after her up the hill. Fine dogs and fine men. I saw them all.

(CHRISTY CLARKE *comes in. He sees the figure on the bed and goes over.*)

CHRISTY : I'm going now, Mister Muskerry. Mister Macnabo . . . Mister Muskerry! Mister Muskerry! Mister Muskerry! Oh, the Master is dead. (*He runs back to the door.*) Mrs. Crilly! Mrs. Crilly! (*He goes back to the bed and throws himself on his knees*). Oh, I'm sorry you're gone, Thomas Muskerry.

OLD PAUPER : And is he gone home, too! And the bees humming and all! He was the best of them. Each of his brothers could lift up their plough and carry it to the other side of the field. Four of them could clear a fair. But their fields were small and poor, and so they scattered.

(MRS. CRILLY *comes in.*)

MRS. CRILLY : Christy Clarke, what is it?

CHRISTY : The Master is dead.

MRS. CRILLY : My God! My God!

CHRISTY : Will I go and tell them below?

MRS. CRILLY : No. Bring no one here yet. We killed him. When everything is known that will be known . . .

CHRISTY : I'll never forget him, I think.

MRS. CRILLY : There seems to be a great humming—I never heard the like of it.

CHRISTY : It's the bees at the window pane. (*He stands listening*). And there's Myles Gorman's pipes on the road.

(*The clear sound of pipes is heard.*)

FINIS